# THE
# REFORM
# OF
# THE
# CHURCH

Other Books by Donald Bloesch

*Centers of Christian Renewal*
*The Christian Life and Salvation*
*The Crisis of Piety*
*The Christian Witness in a Secular Age*
*Christian Spirituality East and West*
(with J. Aumann and T. Hopko)

# THE
# REFORM
# OF
# THE
# CHURCH

BY

DONALD G. BLOESCH

WILLIAM B. EERDMANS PUBLISHING COMPANY
GRAND RAPIDS, MICHIGAN

*To*
DEAN CALVIN SCHNUCKER
AND PROFESSOR JOSEPH MIHELIC
*of Dubuque Theological Seminary*
*in grateful recognition*
*for their friendship and guidance*

## ACKNOWLEDGMENTS

I wish to thank *The Reformed Journal* for granting permission for the republication of the first chapter, "The Need for Biblical Preaching." I am profoundly grateful to Dr. Franklin Littell for writing the foreword and for all his valuable comments and criticisms. I also wish to express my appreciation to my colleague, Dr. Arthur Cochrane, for his helpful suggestions regarding the fifth chapter, "Evangelical Confession." Finally I acknowledge the encouragement of my wife and her aid in the correcting of the manuscript.

# TABLE OF CONTENTS

*The real strength of a Church is not the amount of its work but the quality of its faith. One man who truly knows his Bible is worth more to a Church's real strength than a crowd of workers who do not. — P. T. FORSYTH*

# FOREWORD

Donald G. Bloesch is rapidly taking his place at the front rank of historians and interpreters of the movements toward the renewal of the Church. To his earlier excellent studies — among them *Centers of Christian Renewal* (1964) and *The Crisis of Piety* (1968) for which I am personally grateful — he has now added a major treatment of the reform of the Church.

Sharply critical of popular culture-religion, *The Reform of the Church* begins with "the famine of the Word of God" (Chapter I) and proceeds to discuss the various areas of Christian life in imperative need of reformation. Besides the first chapter, I am especially grateful for Chapter VI on church discipline and Chapter XII on the spiritual disciplines of the Christian life. In an age which exalts "freedom" and makes discipleship cheap and easy, the reminder that the Church is not a "cave of all the winds of doctrine" (Forsyth) nor a free association of the disobedient is most timely.

The author's point of view is soundly Biblical and solidly doctrinal, and in every area he presents critiques and solutions which are grounded in the Word of God and enlivened by informed dialogue with the past. There are two important schools of theological criticism of the prevailing culture-religion in our churches: the writers who say that the Gospel is no longer intelligible or meaningful to "modern man," and the writers who are convinced that the offense of the Gospel is precisely that it is still all too clear and too demanding to be popular. Dr. Bloesch places himself squarely with the latter and evangelical group. This book will therefore be of great usefulness to pastors and laymen who love Christ's Church and who work for a renewal of Christian intellectual discipline and the recovery of a Christian style of life.

The renewed Church which is the author's concern is not a shallow "salvation cult" (Bonhoeffer) devoted to her own interests. On the contrary, the Church is turned outward in prophecy and evangelism and service. Yet Dr. Bloesch is surely correct in criticizing the Church of the liberal social gospel, and the much newer cult of social activism, to the extent that externalization has not been accompanied by the strengthening of the internal disciplines which make a genuine and fruitful church-world dialectic possible. A "church" which has no identity, which is simply devoted to a higher level of culture-religion than the vulgar and prevailing one, has not yet experienced the Baptism of John (repentance) which precedes the Baptism of the Spirit and a new realization of sacramental and liturgical vitality. Neither will it have the blessings of charismatic gifts and spiritual healing which follow on repentance and reformation.

*The Reform of the Church* is a sound and sensitive treatment of the present plight of organized religion, yet it falls into neither of the common false solutions: sectarian flight from responsibility toward the world for which Christ died, or enthusiastic identification with the highest values of the spirit of the times. Dr. Bloesch's book will be studied by theologians and church historians for its scholarly merit. It deserves also to be read and discussed by leaders of the congregations for its practical value.

— FRANKLIN H. LITTELL

# PREFACE

The secularization of the church is one of the key themes of contemporary theology. Whereas the church in the late middle ages sought to subjugate the world, the modern church appears to have surrendered to the world. Many theologians complain that the church today is not sufficiently in the world, but the real problem is that the world is too much in the church. Two theological movements have arisen that seek to meet the challenges that secularism presents to the church — a this-worldly secular theology and an otherworldly sectarian evangelicalism. While the first movement is tempted by syncretism, the second is imperiled by ghettoism. Both signify divergences from the mainstream of the Reformation tradition. We count among the sectarian evangelicals the more extreme dispensationalists and the dominant strand within the charismatic revival, though recognizing that the maturation of the latter movement may hold promise for the future. Those who contend for a theology of revolution and those who see hope primarily in terms of this world are to be included in the general category of secular theology.

In my opinion secular theology presents the greater danger to the life of the church today, since it furthers much more than impedes the process of the secularization of religion. According to this theology the Gospel of Christ is primarily social rather than personal. We are told to seek justice in this world rather than holiness in the world to come. There is a practical equation of creation and redemption, so that history itself has come to be regarded as redemptive. These theologians often appeal to the Bible to substantiate their views, but they forget that the Bible is not simply a book about the world but about the Word of God in the world. They also do not consider that in New Testament religion giving away our faith has priority over giving away our cloak (cf. Ac. 6:1-4). Secular theology reminds us that a religion divorced from the temporal needs and concerns of men can rightly be called the opiate of the people. The New

Social Gospel is a welcome antidote to the older individualism which simply regarded love as the answer to all of man's problems. It is well to recall in this connection Reinhold Niebuhr's dictum: "Love without power simply surrenders the world to power without love." Yet secular theology tends to forget that there can be no abiding social righteousness apart from the spiritual regeneration of persons.

It cannot be denied that in our concern to redress the errors of an older Protestant pietism, we have lost something in the process. Our attention should again be focused upon the full Gospel which is radically personal as well as fully social. We need to hold in balance evangelism and the building of a holy community, individual conversion and nurture and discipline within the church. It is imperative that we recover not only the social passion of the prophets but also the interior life of devotion by which we are given both wisdom and power.

According to Wayne Oates the taboo subject today is no longer sex but rather personal faith. People today, even seminary students, seem ashamed and embarrassed when discussing experiences of God and Christ. The reform of the church in our time will surely entail the recovery of personal faith in the living Savior, Jesus Christ. Nathan Söderblom has declared: "One thing I know — the only religion that now is of any account, the only faith that now can satisfy the deep, questing souls of all tongues and nations, is a new, invincible preaching of the cross; a fresh, convincing experience of the mystery of salvation, revealed in the Saviour's sacrifice of himself in life and death."[*]

Yet there are dangers in an emphasis upon the experiential side of religion. Our trust must be not in our own experience but rather in the objective reality of the cross and resurrection. The answer does not lie in turning inwards, to our own needs and experiences, but rather in losing ourselves in a cause or reality higher than ourselves. Not self-fulfillment but self-transcendence — this has been the need of man ever since the creation. The church too must look beyond itself, beyond its programs and spirituality to the divine Christ who is both its salvation and its judgment. The principal need of our time is not the cultivation of a particular kind of asceticism but the proclamation of the message of reconciliation and redemption in words as well as acts. This is not to deny the place of

---

[*] Nathan Söderblom, "Do We Approach a Renewal of Religion?" Quoted by Gustaf Aulén in *Una Sancta* (Resurrection, 1967), Vol. 24, No. 1, p. 28.

asceticism in the Christian life, but it should be seen in terms
of the service of the Word rather than self-salvation. We uphold
a spirituality of the Holy Spirit whereby men are empowered
to witness to a redemption already procured through the sacrifice of Jesus Christ on the cross. As Forsyth has rightly said:
"Christianity is not the sacrifice we make, but the sacrifice we
trust; not the victory we win, but the victory we inherit. That
is the evangelical principle."**

What we seek is a new kind of evangelicalism, one that is
ecumenical as well as biblical, social as well as personal. While
avoiding the false otherworldliness that disregards life in this
world, characteristic of an introverted "pietism" and much
of Catholic mysticism, we endorse a true otherworldliness that
gives significance to life in this world. The world or the secular
is to be understood neither as a substitute for religion nor as its
enemy but rather as its field of action. The Christian's hope and
goal lie beyond this present world, but he is called to bear
witness to this hope in the very midst of this world. The apostle
admonishes us to work out our salvation in the here and now
(Phil. 2:12; II Cor. 6:2). In this book is set forth a catholic
evangelicalism in contrast to both the radical evangelicalism
of the sects and the secular eclectic theology of the mainline
denominations.

** P. T. Forsyth, *The Justification of God* (London: Independent Press, Ltd.,
1948), pp. 220, 221.

# ONE:

# THE NEED FOR
# BIBLICAL PREACHING

## THE FAMINE OF THE WORD OF GOD

It is becoming more and more common to hear people speak of a famine of the Word of God. As in the days of Amos it would seem that God is withholding His Word in judgment upon a diseased and rebellious civilization. It cannot be denied that there has been a remarkable decline in great preaching since the first World War. The drop in the sales of books of sermons has also been noticeable.

One can certainly speak of a decline in biblical, evangelical preaching. Sermons are still delivered in churches that are often filled, and yet people are not really hearing the Word of the living God. One contemporary prophet has given this description of the situation in Protestant churches:

> Instead of the exposition of the Word of God in the Bible in preaching, laymen are subjected to all manner of speeches, diatribes, commentaries, newscasts, patriotic declamations, poetic recitations, aphorisms, positive thoughts, social analysis, gimmicks, solicitations, sentimentalities, and corn.... The unbiblical tenor of much Protestant preaching is strange, of course, in Protestantism because the opening of the Bible within the congregation was one of the historic promises of the Reformation.[1]

It can be said that modern society exists in a state of spiritual starvation. We have material things in abundance, but we lack the one thing needful — the Word of God. Forsyth has affirmed: "It is not sermons we need, but a Gospel, which sermons are killing."[2] In the opinion of Father Murphy-O'Connor, "the progressive dechristianization of society today" is to be attributed to "a failure of preaching." And he adds that there can be no

---

[1] William Stringfellow, *A Private and Public Faith* (Grand Rapids, Mich.: Eerdmans, 1962), p. 48.

[2] P. T. Forsyth, *The Church and the Sacraments,* 2nd ed. (London: Independent Press, 1947), p. 20.

doubt that "this is due in part to the spiritual mediocrity and
the technical incompetence of individual preachers. . . ."[3]

Among the forms which modern preaching has taken is lectur-
ing on some topic of contemporary cultural import. Such sermons are often known as topical sermons, but they cannot be
regarded as the preaching of the Word of God. They are very
often informative and even edifying, but they do not bring men
the salvation of Christ. They may be illuminating, but they lack
the note of authority. Instead of "thus saith the Lord" people
hear from the pulpit "in my opinion" or "it seems to me."
Topical "preaching" has pervaded the churches of liberal Protestantism.

The homilies which have in the past dominated Roman
Catholic and Anglo-Catholic services have also been "topical"
in character. The pattern of the traditional homily has usually
been moral instruction. Now Catholic theologians are re-examin-
ing the nature of the homily and are defining it as an explana-
tion of a Gospel passage. Yet this still falls short of kerygmatic
preaching which is oriented about the message of the vicarious
death of Christ on the cross and which culminates in a call to
repentance. Some Catholic writers distinguish between homilies
and evangelistic preaching,[4] but all sermons must be evangelistic
in the sense that decision and repentance are necessary even for
Christians, who exist in a state of sin as well as in a state of
grace.

Inspirational speaking is another form of modern preaching
which is also much more cultural than biblical. In the inspirational sermon the purpose is to enliven the congregation, to
stimulate or move them to some creative effort rather than to
give glory to God by upholding His Word. Such preaching is
prone to be more theatrical than evangelical. It is often centered about uplifting personal experiences, and these usually
include the experiences of the speaker. It was Schleiermacher
who maintained that "preaching must always take the form of
testimony . . . to one's own experience."[5] But Paul averred that
we should preach not ourselves but rather Jesus as Lord (II
Cor. 4:5). This is not to deny that authentic biblical preaching
will often serve to inspire and uplift the congregation, but this

---

3 Jerome Murphy-O'Connor, *Paul on Preaching* (N.Y.: Sheed & Ward,
1963), p. xiii.

4 See Dominico Grasso, *Proclaiming God's Message* (Notre Dame, Ind.:
Univ. of Notre Dame Press, 1965), pp. 245-248.

5 Friedrich Schleiermacher, *The Christian Faith*, ed. H. R. Mackintosh and
J. S. Stewart (Edinburgh: T. & T. Clark, 1928), p. 69.

should be seen as a fruit or consequence of the preaching rather than its purpose. Moreover, in this case it is the Word of God that edifies and not the experiences of the minister.

The temptation in both topical and inspirational preaching is to impress upon the hearers one's knowledge and skills rather than to point the people to Jesus Christ. There is also a temptation particularly in scholarly sermonic lectures to address oneself primarily to the intellectuals in the congregation. This is not to denigrate scholarship, but scholarship should be brought into the service of the Word of God, and it should issue in a proclamation that is characterized by both simplicity and profundity. We would do well in this connection to heed the admonition of Philip Spener:

> The pulpit is not the place for an ostentatious display of one's skill. It is rather the place to preach the Word of the Lord plainly but powerfully. Preaching should be the divine means to save the people, and so it is proper that everything be directed to this end. Ordinary people, who make up the largest part of a congregation, are always to be kept in view more than the few learned people, insofar as such are present at all.[6]

Sectarian preaching, which also diverges from the biblical norm, consists in the parroting of a party line. What is regarded as most important is not painstaking exegesis but rather indoctrination and in-group loyalty. It is a particular theological stance that is upheld and not the living Word of God. Sectarian preachers are noted for mouthing clichés rather than bringing a fresh word from the Scripture that challenges the biases of their people. Instead of explicating the Scriptural text they use proof-texts to buttress the officially held doctrinal position. Very often they exult in the "simple Gospel" or the "old-time religion," but this proves upon close examination to be none other than the beliefs and attitudes of their forefathers. Authentic biblical preaching holds up the "full Gospel," the message of the cross related to the cultural and existential situation in which men find themselves.

Finally we are confronted today with the phenomenon known as dialogic preaching in which the preacher seeks not to proclaim a specific message but rather to answer the searching questions of his listeners. In some congregations the minister simply shares his ideas on various questions that are of immediate concern to his people. He sees himself as a fellow seeker

---

6 Philip Jacob Spener, *Pia Desideria*, trans. Theodore G. Tappert (Philadelphia: Fortress Press, 1964), p. 116.

after truth rather than a shepherd of a definite flock. In the coffee house ministry as well as in some other para-parochial ministries dialogic witnessing is very common. The influence of secular theology can be seen in this kind of preaching.

The great majority of sermons today can be categorized as ideological, meaning that they reflect the prejudices and values of the surrounding culture. Ideological preaching is that which absolutizes the particular philosophy and value system which serves the interests of the social group to which the congregation belongs. Types of ideology that are rampant today are the old-time religion, the New Social Gospel, the Reformed Tradition and the American Way of Life. What we have called inspirational speaking is almost always ideology because it tends to reinforce the social bias of the congregation. Preaching that is addressed only to the "inner man" is invariably ideological because it exempts the public sphere of man's life from the criticism of the Word of God. Sectarian preaching is ideological because it enthrones the values and social beliefs of an earlier period in history. The ideologists are false prophets, for they simply mirror the prevailing opinion of the day. They soothe rather than challenge, inspire rather than convert. It can be said that preaching will either be ideological, i.e., it will reflect the values and aspirations of the culture, or it will be biblical and evangelical which means that it will contravene the *Zeitgeist* (the spirit of the times).

What are the reasons for the dearth of biblical preaching in our time? One reason is that ministers are no longer students of the Word and even less theological scholars. They are either unable or unwilling to apply themselves to serious study. They are too immersed in the social life of their communities to become students of Scripture. Again the clergy have for the most part ceased to be men of prayer. Whereas the Puritan pastors in the colonial period would often spend as much as four hours a day in prayer, many ministers have shut prayer out of their lives altogether except for that which is said by rote. Ministers are today suffering from a crisis of identity. They no longer understand their true role. They see themselves as counselors, administrators and public relations men but not as ambassadors of Christ and shepherds of a flock.

The fact that most Protestant clergymen minister to the middle class makes it difficult for them to transcend bourgeois values and prejudices. The high participation of the clergy in service organizations like the Kiwanis, Masons, Rotarians and

Eagles makes them doubly susceptible to ideological contamination, although it must be acknowledged that there are real opportunities for witnessing in such groups.[7] It is no wonder that many Protestant clergy find it impossible to identify themselves with the poor and the outcasts. It is not surprising that in this affluent society there are very few sermons on the evils of gluttony and luxurious living. National sins such as the manufacture of weapons of mass extermination are also seldom exposed from the pulpits of middle and upper class churches. Can it be that much of the language in the pulpit today is meaningless because God is withholding His Spirit in judgment upon men who speak in His name but yet who condone evils which are explicitly condemned in Scripture?

Surely the attempt today to make the faith palatable to its cultured despisers has contributed to the loss of biblical substance in preaching. The temptation to become apologetic, to defend the faith at the forum of reason, is one to which many clergy succumb. Although the truth of faith is intelligible, we tend to forget that the reason of natural man is darkened by sin and therefore incapable of recognizing this truth. To try to embellish the Gospel as if it were a product for sale only cheapens it. Thomas Merton has wisely observed:

> To be dominated by the fear of losing our "hold" on men, especially on youth, is implicitly to confront the world in abject shame at the name and power of Christ. We do not preach Christ, we preach our own modernity, our own cleverness, our liveliness, our fashionableness, and our charm....[8]

### THE HALLMARKS OF BIBLICAL PREACHING

This brings us to the precise nature of biblical preaching. In what way is a biblical sermon different from an ideological sermon or a moral homily? How can we be reasonably certain that we are speaking the Word of God and not simply echoing the views of the culture?

Biblical preaching will first of all be expository. It will seek to explicate a text or passage in Holy Scripture in the light of the Christ revelation. The purpose of preaching is "to make the word of God fully known" (Col. 1:25), and this entails the expounding of Scripture. Illustrations may be used to clarify the meaning of the text, but there is a profound difference

---

[7] It is well to note that such fraternal groups as the Eagles, Moose, Elks and Masons are open only to Caucasians.

[8] Thomas Merton, *Conjectures of a Guilty Bystander* (Garden City, N.Y.: Image Books, Doubleday & Co., Inc., 1968), p. 125.

between theological illustrations and story-telling or reminiscing. Barth says that our purpose should be to interpret the text, not to direct attention away from the text by stories or illustrations. We are called neither to entertain nor captivate our congregations but to confront them with the message of salvation. We are to be *spokesmen* of the Word, not showmen and certainly not salesmen (cf. II Cor. 2:17) .

This brings us to the truth that biblical preaching will be kerygmatic in character. The Greek word *kerygma* signifies the message of redemption. Our purpose should be not simply to uncover the original meaning of the text but to relate this text to the theme of the Bible, the justification of the ungodly. In the words of Louis Bouyer: "It is not for us to make known our own ideas, nor even some abstract doctrine: we have news to tell, the greatest news, the *good* news."[9] We should seek neither to defend nor prove the Gospel but rather to proclaim it intelligibly and lucidly. The Gospel preacher is a herald while the ideological preacher is a propagandist and apologist.

But the ambassador of Christ is called to proclaim not only the divine mercy but also the divine judgment upon the idolatries and transgressions of men. This is to say that he should preach the law as well as the gospel. He is not only to tell what God has done for man in Jesus Christ but also declare what God now requires of man, particularly the man of faith. This means that his preaching should be prophetic as well as kerygmatic.

Prophetic preaching entails specificity and concreteness. It is not enough just to preach against sin. We must unmask the specific sins which plague men and show our hearers how they can make restitution. Reinhold Niebuhr has declared: "The average man is not disturbed when convicted of selfishness as long as he is not told how, when and where he is selfish and his actions are not set in the light of specific alternatives."[10] Neither is it sufficient to uphold Christ or love as the answer to man's predicament. We must point out *how* Christ is the answer and what paths divine love bids us to follow. Much fundamentalist as well as liberal preaching is guilty of the sin of abstractionism; no attempt is made to relate the cross of Christ to the concrete sins of men and nations today. In fundamentalist sermons personal sins are often mentioned but corporate sins are almost

---

9 Quoted in J. D. Benoit, *Liturgical Renewal*, trans. Edwin Hudson (London: SCM Press Ltd., 1958), p. 99.

10 Reinhold Niebuhr, "The Preaching of Repentance," in *The Christian Century* (June 18, 1930), p. 781.

entirely ignored. The weakness in much neo-orthodox (esp. Barthian) preaching is that the kerygma is proclaimed but very little is said about specific transgressions of God's law and the concrete steps men need to take to lead a truly Christian life. The great theologians of neo-orthodoxy are generally exempt from this stricture. Yet there are very few ministers who have been educated in neo-orthodox seminaries who ever preach on the commandment against adultery or the commandment against blasphemy. But must not God's law be proclaimed as well as the message of free grace?

Finally we contend that preaching which is authentically biblical will be doctrinal as well. The reason why many of the great Christian doctrines are not understood by the lay people of the church is that doctrinal matters are often avoided in sermons. To be sure the sermon should be expository and kerygmatic, but can we faithfully explicate Scripture without affirming some doctrine? Our sermons should be proclamations of the good news, but can we truly proclaim the Gospel without committing ourselves to a particular doctrine concerning the atonement or the person of Christ? Doctrine simply makes explicit what is implicit in the Bible and the Christian message. Doctrine safeguards the message of faith and also serves to communicate it. How can we preach the message of salvation without at the same time affirming the doctrine of justification by faith alone?

The distinction that is sometimes made between life-situation and expository sermons is not valid. Every sermon should begin from the Bible and proceed to the cultural situation of men today. The message must be drawn from Scripture, but it must also be directed to the modern world. Barth has rightly maintained that the only two things necessary for a biblical sermon are the Bible and the daily newspaper.

The biblical message will not only break down the walls which divide men, but it will at the same time erect new walls. It overcomes the barriers of class, race and sex, but it creates the new barrier of faith. Whereas it converts the hearts of some, it arouses the opposition of others. This is why Paul could write that the preaching of the Gospel is a savor of death to some and to others an aroma of life (II Cor. 2:15, 16). Yet the minister should beware of trying to create this division and opposition himself. His goal should always be reconciliation and peace among all men. It is the Gospel which creates the division, and this is due not to the express desire of God but to the blindness and stubbornness of men.

## OUR NEED FOR GOD'S WORD AND SPIRIT

Only biblical, evangelical preaching is a means of grace, a means of salvation. In our preaching we bring men not merely information about the reconciling work of God but the very life-giving presence of God. This is conveyed in and through our broken but faithful witness. Barth has written that "there is nothing more important, more urgent, more helpful, more redemptive, and more salutary, there is nothing, from the viewpoint of heaven or earth, more relevant to the real situation than the speaking and the hearing of the *Word* of God...."[11]

One of the dangers in the liturgical movement is that biblical, charismatic preaching might come to be regarded as only one element among others in the divine service, whereas it is an indispensable element. The theme of the liturgical movement is the Word *and* sacrament, and yet it is possible to forget that the dependence of the sacrament upon the Word is much greater than the dependence of the Word upon the sacrament. The sacrament is the culmination of the divine service, but only the Word is absolutely necessary for our salvation. St. Bernardino of Siena put it this way: "If thou canst do only one of these two things, hear the Mass, or hear a sermon, thou shouldst rather leave the Mass than the preaching, for the reason herein expressed, that there is not so much risk to thy soul in not hearing the Mass as in not hearing the sermon."[12]

The plight of the church is that people today generally no longer hear the Word of God. It is true that there are exceptions, since a few pastors filled with the Spirit of God continue to feed their sheep on the bread of life. Yet by and large it would seem that the church is facing a crisis of faith, a dearth of piety. The astounding rise in suicides and alcoholic and dope addiction testifies to the fact that the modern age is engulfed in a vacuum of meaninglessness. People today, even church people, have ceased to have a purpose in life, a self-transcending vision which brings them certainty and fortitude. Victor Frankl, the Austrian psychiatrist, contends that the dominant neurosis today is "noögenic," i.e., it concerns the spirit of man rather than his psyche. The reason why people are afflicted with noögenic neurosis is that they have never heard or no longer hear the Word of God. They are spiritually empty, and their

---

11 Karl Barth, *The Word of God and the Word of Man*, trans. Douglas Horton (N.Y.: Harper & Row, 1957), p. 123.

12 Quoted in Samuel M. Shoemaker, *By the Power of God* (N.Y.: Harper, 1954), p. 128.

shepherds are not feeding them. It is well for us to recall to mind the judgment of God upon the shepherds of Israel who did not feed the sheep or strengthen the weak or heal the sick but instead only fed themselves (Ezek. 34:1-10).

In this time of dearth it might be better to wait and pray for the Spirit of God rather than to place our trust in new promotional schemes or new types of missionary strategy. Perhaps what is needed in a time such as ours is prayer, study and retreat. It has been said that great preaching is born only out of meditation and silence. Bonhoeffer has suggested that we need to pray and serve and wait for God to act in His own time. It is well to remember that Jesus did not begin to preach until He was thirty years of age. St. Paul spent fourteen years in study and meditation before he began his active ministry. What is needed today is a window open to the desert, to the hills which direct us to the spiritual source of our strength (Ps. 121:1). It appears that we need to make contact again with the Spirit of God through prayer and meditation before we can once more preach with power and authority.

# TWO:

# LITURGICAL RENEWAL

The sickness of modern Protestantism can be traced to a loss of the presence of the Holy in our churches. People come to church seeking for the Spiritual Presence, but more often than not they leave the services of worship emptier than when they arrived. According to Langdon Gilkey this loss of the Holy can be detected in conservative as well as liberal forms of Protestantism.[1]

## THE STATE OF WORSHIP IN MODERN PROTESTANTISM

The spiritual apathy of many Christians today can be better understood by examining the state of worship in our churches. What are valued most highly by perhaps a majority of church-goers are uplifting experiences, the fellowship with kindred minds or words of wisdom from the pulpit. Whereas once the glorification of God was considered the primary concern in worship, now it is the fulfillment and welfare of man. Sermons are generally exhortations or expatiations on interesting and sometimes relevant themes. What people are hearing is not the Word of God but the opinions of the minister. The inspiration for his sermons is very often derived not from the Bible but from philosophy and the social sciences.

Worship today can generally be regarded as a rite of cultural religion rather than the service of the glory of God. It is geared to the emotional and religious needs of modern man and not to the great themes of divine judgment and redemption. In this kind of worship it is not the Holy Spirit but the *Zeitgeist* (the spirit of the times) that is encountered. People, moreover, are generally spectators rather than participants in the worship celebration. They come to look and listen but not to present themselves as living sacrifices for the glory of the kingdom of God. Ministers for the most part prove to be lecturers and performers rather than heralds and priests. Choir members

---

[1] See Langdon Gilkey, *How the Church Can Minister to the World Without Losing Itself* (N.Y.: Harper & Row, 1964).

are too often entertainers rather than people who give a special witness to Christ in song. The church service has in too many instances become a religious show or pageant. The church is seen as a dispenser of spiritual vitamins rather than a witness to the grace of God. A great many people come to the church to receive rather than to give glory to God.

Protestant worship has been imperiled by syncretistic theology, which essentially represents the amalgamation of Christian faith and cultural ideology. In culture-Protestantism worship is incurably anthropocentric. It is viewed as a means to self-realization or personal happiness. The cult of "positive thinking" has had a deleterious effect upon Protestant worship. In the more liberal or radical churches worship is seen as a means to realize social ideals, such as the brotherhood of man or peace on earth. Here one can discern the influence of the New Social Gospel movement. The arena of redemption in this kind of theology is no longer the life and death of Jesus Christ but the struggle for social justice and equality. The freedom movement, which is championed by many churchmen, proves to be only another type of folk religion. It represents a new kind of idealism and one that is informed by the message of Scripture. It deserves the support of Christian people, but we must beware of confusing the message of the cross with the message of "freedom now." When we do this we are again in the pitfall of syncretism, even though this may signify an amalgamation with the higher elements of the culture.

But just as the church needs to be wary of syncretism so it must also be on guard against archaism — a retreat into the past. Many of the so-called "high churches" seek to re-create earlier forms of worship. They are characterized by a romantic yearning for the past rather than a sensitivity to the realities of the contemporary situation. The danger in archaistic churches is an obsession with pomp and ceremony. Decorations rather than authentic liturgical symbols are often to be found in such churches.

Another form of archaism is fundamentalism in which the appeal is to sentiment rather than to the Spirit of God. These churches often take pride in defending the "old time religion," but they seem strangely unaware of the fact that they have compromised the Gospel of Jesus Christ by linking it too closely with the values and aspirations of a past cultural epoch. Churches that parade as "confessionalistic" and "orthodox" are often guilty of the same error. Conservative evangelical

Protestants are generally deeply critical of the formal and "liturgical" type of worship; yet they fail to realize that most of their churches too have a fixed or set form of worship and one which is often unalterable.

Closely related to the peril of archaism is ghettoism which signifies isolation from the world. Churches that are preoccupied with form and ceremony often become oblivious to the real world of sin and suffering. Many conservative churches which seek to uphold the God of a particular tradition, such as the Reformed tradition, or of a particular people, such as the American people, are imperiled by ghettoism. Their God is not the God who claims the whole world for His kingdom but rather a tribal god, a god of race, nation or clan. In some of the latter-day pietistic churches, which have actually diverged from historic Pietism, it is not the world that is the theater of redemption (as Calvin averred) but the inner man. And this too can be a form of ghettoism, a means by which we insulate ourselves from the presence of the Holy.

## THE MOVEMENT FOR LITURGICAL REFORM

The liturgical movement has sought to correct the horrendous state of Protestant worship by making the adoration of the living God central again in the lives of the people. Liturgical scholars rightly remind us that liturgy literally means "the work of the people." The object of the liturgical revival is to encourage the participation of the people in the worship experience. What the theologians of this movement have in mind are not only litanies and unison prayers but also lay Scripture reading, the recitation of the creed, congregational singing and most of all frequent participation in Holy Communion.

A secondary purpose of the movement for liturgical worship is to equip the people for mission in the world. The culmination of the worship service is seen to be intercessory and dedicatory prayer. Both of these forms of prayer concern service to the outcasts and unfortunates outside the family of the church. Therefore it can be said that the aim of the liturgical movement is not only the worship of God but the service of God in the world.

Word and sacrament are both regarded as indispensable for liturgical worship. Biblical preaching is stressed almost as much as participation in Holy Communion. The liturgical movement in Protestantism has placed the accent upon the sacrament of the altar primarily because the sacraments have been woefully neglected in main-line Protestantism. The Eucharist moreover is seen by the liturgical theologians not simply as a memorial but as a veritable means of grace, a means by which the people of God are confronted by the real presence of Jesus Christ.

Symbols as aids to worship are highly regarded by the exponents of liturgy. But what they have in mind are not decorations but Christ-centered symbolism, such as the cross, the crucifix or the *Christus Rex*. Indeed, one of the indirect consequences of the movement for liturgical reform has been the stripping away of nonessential symbolism.

In the area of music the emphasis in this movement is on liturgical as over against sentimental music, i.e., music which appeals solely to the emotions. The choir is viewed as a support for the liturgy. The role of the choir is to stimulate and lead congregational singing. In one liturgical church the choir members, who are not robed, sit in the front pews of the congregation.

Again the liturgical reformers seek to recover the priority and centrality of prayer in the service of worship. They stress the importance of intercessory and dedicatory prayer as the fulfillment of the worship celebration. Kneeling and standing are encouraged for prayer rather than sitting. The liturgical movement reminds us that the house of God is to be above all a house of prayer (Is. 56:7; Mt. 21:13).

Finally the movement for liturgical renewal seeks a change in the image of the pastor. The pastor in modern Protestantism has come to be conceived in most churches as a public relations man rather than a shepherd of a definite flock. In many churches he is viewed as a counselor rather than a spiritual director and confessor. The effort to correct this situation can be appreciated by those who are seeking genuine reform in our time. At the same time we must take care not to view the pastor as a divinely ordained mediator between God and the people, for this would mark a return to sacerdotalism.

It is important not to confuse the liturgical movement with the high church movement. Those who are in the vanguard of liturgical reform are much more interested in doctrine than in aesthetics. It is not symbolism and ritual but the service of God's glory that is the paramount concern. Indeed, there is even a Puritanical element in the liturgical movement in that nonessentials, such as ornate windows and irrelevant artistic decorations, are seen as barriers to rather than channels of the grace of God. This is not to deny the fact that there are many in this movement whose primary interest is in vestments, candles, liturgical colors and other liturgical minutiae. But the principal thrust of the movement has thus far definitely been theological.

The liturgical movement has penetrated into all major denominations. It has been strongest in Catholic, Lutheran, Episcopal and French Reformed churches. The Order of St. Luke in the Methodist Church, the Church Service Society in Presbyterian and Reformed churches, the St. Michael's Brotherhood in the Lutheran Church in Germany and the *Una Sancta* magazine, which is edited by Lutherans in the United States, are among the para-parochial groups that are spearheading the drive for liturgical renewal within Protestantism. The movement for liturgical reform is weakest in churches of revivalistic background and community churches. Insofar as the liturgical movement seeks to draw from the riches of the universal church, it has been a powerful aid in the promotion of ecumenicity.

In Roman Catholic churches that have accepted the new liturgical reforms one can discern a definite evangelical strain.[2] First of all the altar has been pushed away from the wall to become an altar table. The priest faces the people in the sacrifice of the mass. There is also a prominent position for the pulpit in some of the liturgically oriented churches. The main part of the mass is now said in the vernacular. Congregational singing has been introduced, and many of the hymns are Protestant in origin. Saints' images have generally been removed including in some cases statues of Mary and Joseph.

A new appreciation of the proclaimed word is also to be discerned in avant garde Roman Catholic churches. The late Cardinal Jules Saliège, who was active in the liturgical movement, devoted one of his last pastoral instructions to the duty of preaching.

> The priest who throws himself with ardour into his work, and yet does not find time to preach, is guilty of a grave dereliction of duty. Christ did not say to his disciples: Put on shows, organize outings. He did not even say: Found orphanages and hospitals. He said: Preach! The apostles understood him well. They left the administration of chanting to the deacons, and devoted themselves to the ministry of the Word.[3]

At the same time there is a noticeable Catholic strain in Prottestant churches which are in the vanguard of the liturgical

---

2 See C. J. McNaspy, *Our Changing Liturgy* (Garden City, N.Y.: Doubleday Image Book, 1967).

3 Quoted in J. D. Benoit, *Liturgical Renewal*, trans. Edwin Hudson (London: SCM, 1958), pp. 104, 105.

movement. What should be mentioned in this connection are a stress on frequent communion, an appreciation of the symbols of the tradition, a rediscovery of the church year, and a reappraisal of private confession. The priesthood of believers is being reinterpreted in its traditional catholic and Reformation sense as the call to be priests to one another rather than each person being his own priest. In liturgical Protestant churches as in their Catholic counterparts, the worship of God and not the personality of the minister is made central.

There is no question that liturgical worship is a great need in our time. Our people are too often spectators rather than participants. Our services revolve too much about the personality of the minister rather than the Word of God. Dr. Torrance has stated the problem well:

> But what has happened in Protestant worship and ministry? Is it not too often the case that the whole life and worship of the congregation revolves round the personality of the minister? He is the one who is in the center; he offers the prayers of the congregation; he it is who mediates "truth" through his personality, and he it is who mediates between the people and God through conducting the worship entirely on his own. Nowhere is this more apparent than in the case of the popular minister where everything centers on him, and the whole life of the congregation is built round him. What is that but Protestant *sacerdotalism*, sacerdotalism which involves the displacement of the Humanity of Christ by the humanity of the minister, and the obscuring of the Person of Christ by the personality of the minister?[4]

## RESERVATIONS CONCERNING THE LITURGICAL MOVEMENT

Our reactions to the movement for liturgical reform are for the most part favorable. This movement is a step in the right direction. It may even be the key to Christian renewal in our time. And yet we have certain reservations.[5]

As has already been mentioned the concern of liturgical leaders is solidly theological and not aesthetic. Yet the temptation to make the artistic concern dominant is very real on the local level. There is a place for symbolism in a Reformed church, since it was Calvin's intention that churches be simple but not barren. Nevertheless a preoccupation with symbolism can de-

---

4 T. F. Torrance, "Justification" in *Christianity Divided*, ed. Daniel J. Callahan, Heiko Oberman and Daniel O'Hanlon (N.Y.: Sheed & Ward, 1961), p. 302.

5 See Donald G. Bloesch, "What's Wrong with the Liturgical Movement?", *Christianity Today* (Jan. 5, 1968), XII, 7, pp. 6, 7.

tract from that which is most important — the preaching and
hearing of the Word of God.

It is a fact that the preference of pastors who lean in the
liturgical direction is for the gothic style of church with its
high ceilings and long narrow nave. The pure gothic form is
not a viable alternative for most congregations because of the
expense involved, but they nevertheless seek to retain the interior arrangement of the gothic church including the divided
chancel and central altar. The gothic type of church certainly
contradicts the Reformation conception of the church as a
family of believers congregated to hear the Word and partake
in the fellowship meal.

In a church that seeks to remain true to the Evangelical
Reformation acoustics is of supreme importance. Yet in many
liturgical churches the pulpit is placed so far to the side that
the word of the sermon is often not heard by the people. The
facing of the pastor toward the altar (or altar table) in prayer
also is very bad acoustically and ipso facto theologically as well,
since both the prayer and the sermon should be heard by the
people.[6] Our recommendation is for the pulpit to be given
a central position (although not necessarily one in mid-center),
so that there can be direct eye and ear contact between pastor
and people.

Liturgical churches need to be on guard against formalism as
well as aestheticism. Liturgical worship partly because it calls
for the corporate participation of the people will have a definite form or pattern. A structured pattern of worship is certainly preferable to worship which has no specific pattern or
direction. Paul recommended that "all things should be done
decently and in order" (I Cor. 14:40). Yet Paul also warned
against binding or quenching the Spirit (I Thes. 5:19, 20). An
overreliance upon pericopes allows for no direct guidance by
the Spirit in the selection of the Scripture reading and text.
The church lectionary should be only a general guide, not an
indefeasible criterion. The charismatic element must be channeled but not stifled. This brings us to the subject of ritual
prayer which is an ever-present danger in liturgical churches.
There is certainly a place for formal prayer in unison, but this
must not obscure the important role of free prayer. Karl Barth

---

[6] Another objection to the practice of the pastor facing the altar with his
back to the people for the general prayers is that this creates the impression
in the minds of many that God is somehow more present on the altar than
in the fellowship of the congregation. This is a Roman Catholic but not an
Evangelical conception.

maintains that the pastoral prayer must be carefully prepared, but it should be said rather than read.

Another sign of formalism is the decline of heartfelt singing on the part of the people. Despite the fact that the liturgical theologians speak of the need for congregational participation in the musical side of worship, choirs often take the place of congregational singing in liturgical churches. The complex nature of many of the "new hymns" in our hymnals tends to discourage congregational singing. At the same time the liturgical experts are right when they warn against sentimental hymns, i.e., hymns that are geared primarily to the feelings of people rather than to the message of Scripture. This is not to deny the rightful place for hymns that edify man as well as give glory to God. Indeed there is a place for both subjectivistic and objectivistic hymns; we need to draw our hymns from a variety of traditions not excluding the American Gospel tradition. The prime purpose of our hymns should be to exalt Jesus Christ, but a concern for and joy in our salvation does not necessarily take glory away from Christ. Perhaps brass bands and piano as well as organ accompaniment might promote genuine congregational singing. But we must beware of liturgical gimmicks that mix showmanship and religion.[7]

It should also be said that the liturgical revival has not yet rectified the sad state of preaching in our churches (both Protestant and Catholic). Some of those who are active in this movement have proved to be earnest biblical preachers, but the bane of formalism has also made itself felt in the ministry of the Word. Charismatic, evangelical preaching is one of the goals that have yet to be realized in liturgical churches. And this means that a liturgical worship that is both catholic and evangelical is, for the most part, still an ideal and not an accomplished fact.

Finally we must warn of the danger of introversion in the movement for liturgical renewal. The worship experience rather than the great themes of reconciliation and redemption might come to be regarded as basic. Our attention might become so focused upon the cultus that we lose sight of the church's mission to the world. To the credit of liturgical theologians

---

[7] In our view liturgical jazz belongs in the category of entertainment and showmanship. Jazz is meant to be listened and danced to rather than sung. Also because it reflects the meaninglessness and brokenness in modern culture, it cannot serve as a vehicle for God's Word to the same degree as, for example, authentic folk songs which still mirror the goodness of God's creation.

they are generally aware of the hazard of introversion or ghettoism and constantly remind their hearers that the worship of
God must be integrally related to the service of our fellowman.

Part of the trouble in the liturgical movement within Protestantism is that Catholic practices are simply being aped rather
than scrutinized in the light of the Word of God. It is well to
bear in mind that the very meaning of liturgy is different in
Reformation theology from what it is in Roman Catholicism.
In evangelical Protestant theology liturgy signifies the service
of God in proclamation and thanksgiving. In Roman Catholic
theology liturgy means sacramental worship which is partly
propitiatory in character. The culmination of the liturgy in
Catholic churches is the offering of Christ to the Father in the
sacrifice of the mass. Liturgical worship in Protestantism on the
other hand signifies the witnessing to the finished sacrifice of
Christ in the sermon and the sacrament.

This is not to deny that the theology of worship is being rethought today by scholars in both Protestant and Roman traditions. Protestant theologians such as Gustaf Aulén now believe
that it is possible to speak of a Eucharistic sacrifice.[8] He contends
that although we cannot offer Christ we certainly can plead
His sacrifice to the Father. And we must definitely offer a sacrifice of praise and thanksgiving which is united with Christ's
intercessory sacrifice at the right hand of God. Catholic scholars
on the other hand are pointing to the truth that the mass has
no real efficacy apart from the preaching of the Word. C.
Vagaggini has written: "Without the ministry of the Word,
the rite runs the risk of being fruitless for the faithful who
do not understand its meaning and do not bring to it the necessary moral disposition."[9] Perhaps there is hope for some real
breakthroughs in this area, since Protestant and Catholic thinkers seem to be converging towards some new or fresh understanding of liturgical worship.

Protestantism today stands in need of liturgical renewal. There
is something wrong in churches which adulate Mother's Day
but ignore Maundy Thursday and Good Friday. There is also
something amiss when people partake of Communion only once
or twice a year, whereas genuinely catholic worship is not com-

---

8 See Gustaf Aulén, *Eucharist and Sacrifice* (Philadelphia: Muhlenberg,
1956).

9 Quoted in Dominico Grasso, *Proclaiming God's Message* (Notre Dame:
Univ. of Notre Dame Press, 1965), p. 119.

plete apart from it. This does not mean, however, that the Eucharist is necessary on every worship occasion.

At the same time we must not regard any particular liturgy as sacrosanct or normative. The liturgical renaissance will be a source of renewal if it encourages liturgical diversity and allows for a greater degree of spontaneity in the services of worship. To make the ancient liturgies the criterion for authentic worship can be dangerous. We need to heed the warning of Frederick Schroeder:

> Just as there is a diversity of gifts within the church, so there should be a diversity of liturgical forms, if for no other reason than to serve people of different temperaments and traditions. There is no biblical precedent or theological justification for any one form of worship . . . . no attempt should be made to force the church into some kind of liturgical straitjacket. Cultural rigidity has repeatedly eventuated in formalism, ceremonialism, and a loss of religious vitality.[10]

It is our view that liturgical renewal will not come until the Word of God is rightly proclaimed and obeyed and Holy Communion again becomes supremely important in the lives of the people. But Holy Communion should not be seen as a magical rite but rather as a fellowship meal which transcends the barriers of race, class and denomination. Moreover, the Word is not rightly obeyed until we seek to do the will of God in the public areas of life as well as the private, and this entails identification with the tribulation of the outcasts and underdogs of society.

The presence of the Holy will not be restored in our churches by the creation of a worshipful mood or by beautifying the worship sanctuary. Rather the Holy will be present to us when we seek to obey the Holy God in every area of life and give Him glory before all men. We need again to pay heed to the words of Hosea: "For I desire steadfast love and not sacrifice, the knowledge of God, rather than burnt offerings" (Hos. 6:6). The prophet was not protesting against the temple cultus as such but rather against its perversion which took the form of a ceremonialism devoid of ethical content. The Holy will be present in a church that is willing to stand against the stream of the culture on such matters as the manufacture of nuclear armaments, sexual promiscuity and perversion, and racial discrimination. When the church seeks not to preserve and beautify itself but rather to lose itself for the glory of God in service to

---

[10] Frederick W. Schroeder, *Worship in the Reformed Tradition* (Philadelphia: United Church Press, 1966), p. 148.

the world, then God will once again send forth His Spirit upon His people. What is needed is not ceremony and ostentation but a zeal for social righteousness and a passion for the salvation of the lost. If liturgical renewal entails moral renewal, if it prepares the way for a true spiritual awakening, then it will serve the cause of a revitalized Christian church in our time.

# THREE:

# THE CRISIS OF BAPTISM

### THE LOSS OF MEANING IN THIS SACRAMENT

The sacrament of holy baptism is now under scrutiny by both Protestants and Catholics. Some theologians, such as Karl Barth and Emil Brunner, have spoken of the scandal of infant baptism. They deplore the fact that baptism has so often become separated from a living faith in Jesus Christ. Harvey Cox reinterprets baptism as a pledge and dedication to social righteousness. Tom Torrance and Max Thurian contend that the need is to recover the reality of the action of God in this sacrament.

Church theologians are becoming increasingly aware that although the majority of people still demand baptism for their children, this rite has become emptied of all real meaning. The Bishop of Wakefield, J. A. Ramsbotham, expresses the growing concern of many church leaders: "Speaking only for the Church of England, would I be wrong to say that 90 per cent of the members have gone through the motions of infant baptism, some kind of religious upbringing, confirmation, even perhaps first confession and first communion, but have not in fact gone through the baptismal experience of dying and of being raised again, of condemnation and of being justified."[1]

At its worst baptism, particularly infant baptism, is a social convention. What is regarded as important is not the electing grace of God nor the moment of decision but rather the naming of the child. It is a rite not of the new birth but of natural birth.

Some progress has been made when baptism is viewed as a ceremony of dedication. Then it becomes a means by which the child or believer is accepted into the family of the church. Its relation to personal faith is more clearly seen, but this is still not the biblical understanding of this sacrament. Forsyth has rightly affirmed: "To treat Baptism as a mere ceremony of reception into the Church and of addition to its rolls does

---

[1] Basil S. Moss, ed., *Crisis for Baptism* (London: SCM, 1965), p. 46.

what its treatment as a mere dedication of an infant also does — it destroys it as a Sacrament."[2]

It cannot be doubted that baptism, like many other rites of the church, has become an occasion for cheap grace. It is a means by which grace is freely dispensed but without requiring anything in return. It should demand from the believer his very life, but instead it costs him nothing nor does it place any great burden of responsibility upon the parents or god-parents.

The erosion of the biblical significance of this sacrament can be seen in the Roman Catholic church where the rite itself is believed to effect salvation *(ex opere operato)*. According to Catholic theology original sin is washed away at baptism, although the inclination to sin remains. The baptized child is said to receive infused faith and love, but such faith is distinguished from the act of faith which comes later. Among many Roman Catholics there is an almost magical, mechanical understanding of the sacrament of baptism. Official Catholic theology seeks to guard against such a misunderstanding by holding that for baptism to be valid the right intention must be present on the part of the priest, the believer and the community of faith.

Among some branches of high church Lutheranism and Anglicanism baptism is also viewed as a rite which effects regeneration even in the case of infants. Some Lutherans, in a manner similar to Roman Catholics, speak of a disposition to faith or implicit faith in the baptized infant. Baptism in this kind of theology is a guarantee of salvation, a ticket to heaven. But any doctrine of instant salvation particularly when related to the sacrament of baptism becomes an occasion for cheap grace. It is to be recognized that both Luther and Calvin held to baptismal grace, but they did not believe that regeneration is fully effected at baptism. In their view sin continues within the baptized Christian although guilt is no longer imputed. Moreover, personal faith is necessary if baptism is to be fully effective for salvation.

In classical Reformed Christianity baptism is viewed as the sign and seal of the covenant which God has made with His people and whose benefits also extend to their children. There is biblical foundation for this position, and yet if it is interpreted in a certain way it also becomes a medium of cheap grace. We come to believe that people are born into the kingdom by virtue of having Christian parents. But no one is born a Chris-

---

2 P. T. Forsyth, *The Church and the Sacraments*, 2nd ed. (London: Independent Press, 1947), p. 193.

tian; no infant is ever baptized a Christian. We are baptized towards the Christian faith, or, as Calvin said, toward future repentance and faith, but we are not automatically Christians. A Christian home makes it possible for us to hear the message of faith, but no one can believe for anyone else.

In liberal Protestantism baptism is the means by which we are counted and recognized as children of God. In the thinking of such theologians as Maurice we are already sons of God by virtue of our creation in His image. According to Horace Bushnell the child is by nature Christian, and he ought to grow up into Christianity naturally just as he grows up into citizenship. But we then lose sight of the truth that we are adopted into the kingdom by repentance and faith. Our Lord said that we enter the kingdom by violence (Lk. 16:16), and this biblical theme of crisis and struggle must not be overlooked.

The practice of private baptisms, that is, baptisms apart from the worship of the believing community, has further subverted the biblical and catholic basis of this sacrament. By separating baptism from the community of faith, the very symbolism of the sacrament as an entrance into the church of Jesus Christ is called into question. When priests and ministers are paid for such baptisms, the pagan idea of buying one's way into heaven makes its reappearance.

Karl Barth maintains that the modern church has lost sight of the ground of baptism, namely, the death and resurrection of Jesus Christ. Unless we discern the integral connection between baptism with water and participation in the death of Christ, we no longer know what baptism is. According to Barth both an emphasis on *ex opere operato* and on an overt experience of conversion obscure the ground and source of the efficacy of baptism.

Another contributing factor in the demise of baptism in the modern world is that it is separated from the work of the Holy Spirit in faith. Cullmann speaks of the gift of God in the act of baptism, but he links this gift to the rite itself rather than to faith.[3] He also refers to a general baptism of Christ for all men independent of the faith of those who benefit from it.[4] Yet we are not remaining true to Scripture unless we recognize that there is no baptismal efficacy apart from the obedience of faith.

---

[3] Oscar Cullmann, *Baptism in the New Testament*, trans. J. K. S. Reid (London: SCM, 1950), pp. 33, 49, 52.

[4] *Ibid.*, pp. 19, 20, 33, 70.

The biblical, theological meaning of baptism has been lost in the minds of most people today, but it still retains a cultural meaning and perhaps also a magical meaning. It is related to the supernatural in a vague sense, but its witness to the historical atonement of Jesus Christ is no longer discerned. It is regarded as a social necessity but not as a momentous spiritual occasion which determines one's very destiny. It is still very often seen as an act which has significance for membership in the church, but that it is an effectual sign of dying and rising again from the dead is simply not comprehended by most Christians today.

The loss of the catholic substance of this sacrament also extends to believers' baptism. Baptism in revivalist churches is a symbol not of the death of Jesus Christ but of an experience of conversion. It is related to faith but not to the election of God revealed and fulfilled in the cross of Christ. In perhaps a majority of Baptist churches the sacrament of baptism has a purely subjective, cultural meaning. In many circles it is no longer seen even as a sacrament but simply as an ordinance of the church. Because it assures the convert that he is accepted by God and the family of the church, it again prepares the way for cheap grace.

### REINTERPRETING BAPTISM

We shall recover the deeper significance of baptism only when we recognize it as a sacrament and not simply as a dedicatory ceremony. It is a divine ordinance, instituted by Jesus Christ for our salvation (Mt. 28:19, 20). St. Augustine defined a sacrament as a visible sign of an invisible grace. Certainly baptism is such a sign, but it has no efficacy apart from divine grace. Otherwise it would be on the same level as a magical rite.

Baptism is a sign of our death and resurrection in Jesus Christ. But it is not an empty symbol but rather an effectual sign. This is to say, it conveys what it signifies. It is a means by which we die and rise with Christ. It is a means by which we participate in His death and resurrection (Rom. 6:3, 4; Col. 2:12). It has not simply to do with the *cognito salutis* (the assurance of salvation) but with the *causa salutis* (the cause of salvation). Peter called his hearers to repent and "be baptized ... for the remission of sins" (Ac. 2:38). Barth errs when he sees baptism only in connection with the knowledge of salvation and not with the concrete realization of this salvation in the lives of men.

The components of baptism, as Calvin already clearly perceived, are the shed blood of Christ, the gift of the Spirit,
water, the word and faith. By the word we mean not only
the promise of Christ in Scripture but the proclamation of this
promise in the church. Scripture tells us that the baptismal rite
is not fulfilled apart from the preached word (Eph. 5:26). Nor
is it efficacious apart from faith (Mk. 16:16; Col. 2:12).

In this sacrament one can discern two poles. First there is
the objective work of God in Christ which is signified by the
water. Then there is the gift of the Spirit which brings about
faith. Baptism is not complete unless both dimensions are present — the electing grace of God and the personal acceptance
of our vocation in faith.

In line with the historic Catholic position we affirm the reality
of baptismal grace. The Holy Spirit is truly working in baptism
so long as God's Word is proclaimed and the water is administered in the name of the triune God. Yet we hold that baptismal grace does not signify the fullness of regeneration but only
the commencement of our regeneration. The rite of baptism
does not insure or guarantee regeneration, for otherwise we are
again confronted with the peril of cheap grace. Because the Holy
Spirit is at work even in infant baptism, we can affirm that a
thirst for salvation is awakened within the recipient even though
faith itself may not yet be present. The baptized child begins
to seek for salvation, but seeking is not yet believing. In contradistinction to Catholic theology we hold that a disposition
towards God is not yet faith. Faith is to be understood as
heartfelt confidence and trust in Jesus Christ, and apart from
faith one is not yet a member of His church. Baptism places
us on the doorway to the kingdom, but we ourselves must take
the final step of entry into the kingdom, and no one, not even
our parents, can believe for us.

Baptism is a rite of initiation, but it does not encompass the
whole of salvation. It is viewed by Paul as the circumcision of
Christ (Col. 2:11, 12), and this means that it is a beginning.
Luther was keenly aware that the real struggle in working
out our salvation lies after our baptism. He declared:

> But we should note that it is not necessary that all be found
> in this state of perfection as soon as they are baptized into this
> kind of death. For they are baptized "into death," i.e., toward
> death; in other words: they have taken only the first steps
> toward the attainment of this death as their goal.[5]

5 Martin Luther, *Luther: Lectures on Romans,* ed. and trans. Wilhelm
Pauck (Philadelphia: Westminster, 1961), p. 181.

To be sure Luther also made many statements that verge towards sacramentalism and that seem to open the door again to "easy salvation." We need only consider the following: "Baptism makes a man once for all and completely pure and blessed, so that there is nothing lacking for the title or heritage of blessedness than such faith in the mercy of such a God."[6] But it must be noted that he does not here separate baptism from faith. Moreover, for Luther our purity is not in ourselves but in Christ, and thereby he is able to avoid the peril of perfectionism.

Some theologians today seek to give up the practice of infant baptism, but we do not subscribe to this line of thought. Infants are to be baptized because children too are claimed for the kingdom of God (Mt. 10:14; Lk. 18:16). Also the New Testament tells us that the apostles baptized entire households (Ac. 16:15, 33; 18:8; I Cor. 1:16). We should only bear in mind that the rite of baptism apart from faith does not effect regeneration.

This brings us to the relation between baptism and the new birth. In the New Testament baptism is often associated with the cleansing work of the Holy Spirit (Ac. 2:38; 22:16; Eph. 5:26; Tit. 3:5). In the latter verse it is described as "the washing of regeneration and renewal in the Holy Spirit." Water baptism is the sign and seal of the new birth, the baptism with the Holy Spirit.

This does not mean, however, that baptism with water and the Spirit occur simultaneously. We affirm only that there is an integral spiritual relation between baptism by water and the gift of the Spirit. The two are tied together not because of any sacred quality of the water but because of the promise of Jesus Christ.

The relation between the two types of baptism can be made clear by the illustration of a surgical operation and an anesthetic. The patient who is dying of the cancer of sin needs to be operated by the Spirit of God, and an anesthetic (baptism) is the proper way to prepare for it. The real operation is invisible, since it involves the inward cleansing of man's heart. Yet this does not mean that the visible sign, baptism, is only an appendage to the operation; it is indeed a highly important ingredient which facilitates the operation. But it is possible to be baptized with the Spirit apart from water baptism, just as an anesthetic is not absolutely necessary in a surgical operation.

---

[6] Luther, *Werke* (Weimar, 1883ff.), 10, I, 112.

Again we come to the truth that baptism and faith belong together. In line with the above illustration the patient must freely submit to the operation or else it cannot be performed. The submission to the anesthetic and the operation, of course, comprises a part of the operation itself, and we could not surrender unless our will was already being converted by the Spirit.

When we speak of faith we have in mind personal faith primarily and the faith of the parents and the church secondarily. This does not mean that the latter are unimportant, since the faith of the new convert cannot grow except in the community of faith which is the church. Also in the case of infant baptism the child is brought to the church by parents who believe, and unless the child is baptized into the community of the church the yearnings for God within the child will never materialize into faith. We must steadfastly affirm against some Lutherans and Catholics that faith itself is not given in infant baptism. At the same time we hold that grace in baptism makes faith possible. Baptized infants should probably be regarded as pre-Christians who may or may not become full-fledged Christians.

In this new ecumenical climate the sacrament of baptism is being radically rethought by Catholic theologians, and many of them are coming to see the indispensability of personal faith. Father Jerome Murphy-O'Connor reflects this ecumenical viewpoint:

> Without faith . . . baptism is void, producing no fruit; and without preaching, there can be no faith. . . . The saving power of baptism is not given it by the faith of the recipient; however, his attitude of entire submission is a condition *sine qua non* that the sacrament produce its effects.[7]

We should go on to affirm that just as faith is necessary for the completion of baptism, so faith also seeks baptism for its fulfillment. Dr. D. T. Niles tells of a Hindu convert who continually postponed his baptism because of the opposition of his family.[8] He finally fell back into the old faith because he was not willing to declare his allegiance to Jesus Christ publicly in the act of baptism. One might say that his new birth was consequently aborted.

Perhaps in this new ecumenical age a breakthrough is near

[7] Jerome Murphy-O'Connor, *Paul on Preaching* (N.Y.: Sheed & Ward, 1963), pp. 15, 20.

[8] Daniel T. Niles, *The Context In Which We Preach* (Geneva: John Knox House Association, 1956), p. 11.

whereby the church can do justice once again to the objective
reality of baptismal grace and the subjective necessity for personal surrender and decision. The Reformed church has stressed
*nullum sacramentum sine fide,* which means that there is no
sacrament apart from faith. We can still hold to this today provided it is not taken to mean that our faith creates the presence
of Christ in the sacrament. Indeed it may become possible for
an Evangelical to accept with certain reservations the Catholic
concept of *ex opere operato* particularly if this is now interpreted to mean *ex opere Christi,* by the work of Christ.[9]

In order to guard against a magical understanding of baptism
it is necessary that proper education be given the baptized child
concerning his responsibility to respond to God's grace. He
should be led by his superiors towards repentance and decision.
This decision, however, should not be equated with confirmation, since confirmation presupposes the new birth. Baptism
alone is the sign of such a decision, but the decision itself usually
takes place in the solitariness of one's chamber although never
apart from the community of faith.

There is a need today to relate baptism to church discipline.
The time has come to end indiscriminate baptism. The church
should agree to administer this sacrament only to those who
openly confess faith in Jesus Christ or whose parents make such
a confession. Parents also need to be educated so that they might
give more serious consideration to their vows to bring up their
children in the nurture and admonition of the Lord. The pastor
should conduct special classes with all parents who seek baptism
for their children and instruct them concerning the solemn
character of this sacrament. If either one of the parents is not
a member of the church, then he or she should not be permitted to take vows on the child's behalf; but this does not
preclude the parent from standing up for the child as a witness.

This brings us to the subject of godparents. In some churches,
such as the Presbyterian, the congregation makes a promise to
instruct the child in the ways of God. When the churches were
still small, closely-knit congregations as in the frontier days,
there was good reason for giving this responsibility to the congregation, since everyone knew everyone else. But in this age
of urbanization and mechanization, when no one family is
acquainted sufficiently with another in the church to make it
feasible for caring directly for the spiritual welfare of every

---

9 See Paul Empie and William Baum, eds., *Lutherans and Catholics in
Dialogue,* II (N.Y.: National Lutheran Council, 1967), p. 67.

child, the custom of congregational pledges in this respect is
ludicrous if not blasphemous. Our recommendation is to have
godparents, i.e., consecrated Christians who know the family of
the child intimately and who would be in a position to give
spiritual guidance to the child. This practice too has become
suspect particularly when the godparents are chosen on the basis
of family ties rather than spiritual maturity. So often godparents
are selected for the purpose of providing for the physical welfare
of the children if something should happen to their parents.
But the prime purpose of the godparent is to be a spiritual
director and confessor. Godparents too should be approved by
the pastor and in some cases even by the session of the church,
and they also should be given special instruction by the pastor
concerning the meaning of baptism and their obligations to
the child.

Concerning the mode of baptism the richest symbolism is
immersion in water, but this is not practical for infants. In
the case of infants or small children our recommendation is
that the water be poured upon their heads from a pitcher,
since pouring symbolizes the descent of the Spirit. The water
should, of course, first have been taken from the font. For an
adult we would leave the decision as to the precise mode of
baptism to him. Some theologians suggest a threefold pouring
thereby making it solidly trinitarian, but either way conveys
the meaning. One should recognize that there is nothing magical in the use of water, but at the same time it should be
acknowledged that water in unison with the Word is the means
by which Christ has chosen to seal His regenerating grace in
the hearts of men.

Christian renewal will come about when the church recovers
the biblical and catholic meaning of this sacrament. We do not
need a new sacrament, such as Penance, which supplements
baptism. Nor do we need a new experience, such as the Pentecostal experience, if it is seen as something quite different from
or higher than the experience of faith. Our task is to return to
our baptism, that is, to the faith into which we were baptized.
Our need is to reappropriate the fruits of our baptism. Our
baptism can be fruitful only in a life of daily repentance under
the cross. Only then does it mark our entry into the kingdom of
God. Only then does it attest the fact that we have been buried
with Christ on Calvary and that we have risen with Him through
the power of His Spirit.

FOUR:

# THE CENTRALITY
# OF THE EUCHARIST

## THE STATUS OF THE SUPPER TODAY

It was P. T. Forsyth who declared, "Sacraments, not socialities, make the center of our church life and social unity."[1] Yet in the life of modern Protestantism it would seem that dinners and committee meetings comprise the bond of unity. Even in Roman Catholicism where the sacraments and particularly the mass have such high official status, on the popular level novenas, shrines and raffles are given much more attention. But if the sacraments are the divinely given flying buttresses which save the church from collapse (Emil Brunner), then we should again recognize their rightful place within the life of the church. And the Lord's Supper, which is integrally related to the whole of Christian worship, needs especially to be given serious consideration if church renewal is to become a reality in our time.

If one surveys the situation in Protestantism today it will be seen that the sacrament of the Lord's Supper has lost much of its catholic and biblical meaning. In many churches this sacrament is nothing more than a memorial rite. This perhaps accounts for the marked solemnity and lack of joy in the celebration of this rite. And it should be noted that there is an infrequent observance of the Lord's Supper in most Protestant churches, including Lutheran and Anglican. The situation has improved since the seventeenth and eighteenth centuries when in the English-speaking world the rite was usually celebrated only twice a year. Interestingly enough in England there was more frequent observance of the supper in the free churches than in the Anglican church. Another thing to be deplored is the practice of indiscriminate communion. Unlike the churches of the Reformation and Puritanism, modern Protestantism with few exceptions makes no attempt to discipline unruly or factious

---

[1] P. T. Forsyth, *The Church and the Sacraments*, 2nd ed. (London: Independent Press, 1947), p. 224.

brethren by withholding the elements. Moreover, in many denominations such as the Churches of Christ, the Disciples of
Christ, and to a lesser extent the Methodist, even tiny children
are admitted to the Lord's Supper despite the fact that they
are unable to discern His body and blood. Sometimes Communion is given even to the unbaptized thus again ignoring
the warning of the apostle that those who eat and drink without
discerning the body bring judgment upon themselves (I Cor.
11:29). Finally it should be recognized that a strong subjectivistic element is present in Protestant Eucharistic worship. Even
in sacramental churches, such as the Lutheran and Episcopal,
it is not the objective reality of the risen Christ but rather the
inward spiritual experience that is deemed most important.[2]

On the Roman Catholic side the original meaning of the
sacrament has also been at least partly subverted. In many
Roman churches the sacrament is seen as a semi-magical rite
in which the bread and wine are miraculously changed by
the words of the priest. The priest is viewed more as a miracle
worker than as a herald. The presence of Christ in the sacrament is conceived as impersonal and static rather than personal
and dynamic. Moreover, many Catholics, in some countries the
majority, come to the church to witness the miracle of the
mass rather than to participate in Holy Communion. They are
spectators, not participants, something which the liturgical movement within the Roman church is now seeking to correct. Countless numbers of Catholics seek to adore the host, and this has
become a rival form of devotion to Communion. Again the conception of the mass as a sacrifice is not without its dangers particularly if this is conceived of as an extension or repetition
of the sacrifice of Christ on Calvary. The practice of private
masses, communion under one species only, and the idea of the
mass as a meritorious work also contravene the biblical understanding of this sacrament.

It is a matter of conjecture whether the position of the sac-
rament is more intact in Catholic or in Protestant churches.
In the words of the English Congregationalist John Whale:
"Discerning minds are now asking from which of two abuses
Christendom will turn out to have suffered more — the corrupt
and superstitious use of the sacramental principle within
Catholicism which inevitably provoked the Protestant protest:
or the blind and continuous iconoclasm within Protestantism

---

2 We here have in mind the popular thinking on this matter and not the
official view of these churches.

which has now come near to destroying the sacramental foundation of Christianity altogether, and therewith the religious basis of its own protest."[3] Perhaps we should say that the danger of anti-sacramentalism is greater than that of sacramentalism, since what is ossified or perverted can be restored again to life but what has been dissolved is no longer in existence.

In order to counteract the secularization of this rite, Protestant and Catholic scholars today are seeking to recover its theological significance. Evangelical theologians who have sought to reinterpret the sacrament of the Lord's Supper are Torrance, Aulén, Thurian, Donald Baillie, Whale, Wyon, and Karl Barth. Such men as Aulén and Donald Baillie are rediscovering the element of sacrifice in the Eucharist. They are also treating the Eucharist as a means of grace, a channel of salvation.

In the Roman Catholic church also there have been fresh and exciting reappraisals of the meaning of the Lord's Supper. We should mention in this connection the contributions of such theologians as Schillebeeckx, Cooke, Diekmann, Haering, Schoonenberg and Rahner. Catholic theologians are affirming that it is unbiblical to speak of a repetition or extension of the Calvary sacrifice in the mass. They are stressing the need for Holy Communion and not merely witnessing the mass. They are also contending that *ex opere operato* must not be understood mechanically but rather personally. The real meaning of this term according to such men as Schillebeeckx and Diekmann is *ex opere Christi,* by the work of Christ. These theologians are also pointing to the necessity of personal faith if the sacrament is to be efficacious for our salvation. Schillebeeckx has declared:

> From this we see that the sacraments do not work automatically, but rather that, as a result of faith and a deep religious longing, they lay hold of the sanctifying power of Christ which is at work in the sacramental Church. But this grasping of salvation in faith is actually the person's *being grasped* by the redeeming Christ.[4]

The presence of Christ in the Eucharist is also being reinterpreted in Catholic theology today. It is being understood in terms of personal encounter rather than the transmutation of substance. The doctrine of transubstantiation is not being

---

3 John Whale, *Victor and Victim* (Cambridge University Press, 1960), p. 138.

4 E. H. Schillebeeckx, "The Sacraments: An Encounter with God" in *Christianity Divided*, eds. Daniel Callahan, Heiko Oberman and Daniel O'Hanlon (N.Y.: Sheed & Ward, 1961), p. 269.

refuted, but it is now being reinterpreted in some circles as transignification and transfinalization. This is to say, what is changed in the Communion service is the purpose or signification of the bread and wine, which is close to the Aristotelian meaning of "substance." In this connection the idea of the localized presence of Christ in the elements is being called into question. The Dutch Jesuit Schoonenberg has stated that Christ's presence primarily means not Christ's body being there in the species but Christ's presence in the eucharistic community. Bernard Cooke has declared: "Strictly speaking the risen Christ cannot be said to be in any place in our world. It is more accurate to speak of him as being present *to* a place, since no spatial situation can either contain or limit him."[5] It should be recognized that many of these interpretations which are deemed radical by conservative churchmen, are actually restatements of truths that are solidly anchored in the catholic tradition of the church. For example, even at the time of the Reformation the Franciscan scholar Kaspar Schatzgeyer asserted that Christ is not in the sacrament "in natural form" but "in a spiritual manner." Like the scholars today he did not deny transubstantiation, but he sought to give an interpretation of this doctrine in terms that would do justice to the total biblical and catholic witness.

## THE WITNESS OF THE REFORMATION

Before we seek to give a reinterpretation of our own, it is well to recall the Reformation understanding of the Eucharist. As Protestants we cannot afford to ignore the contributions of the Reformation in any area of theology, since we seek an understanding of the church that is Evangelical and Reformed as well as Catholic.

Luther's approach to Eucharistic theology marked a significant departure from traditional Catholic thought. His emphasis was on Holy Communion and not the sacrifice of the mass. He held, however, that in Communion we participate in Christ's sacrifice. We receive the fruits of Christ's sacrifice and indeed the very presence of Christ. He understood the real presense in terms of a dynamic event. Christ makes Himself present "in, with and under" the elements of bread and wine, and thereby He can be manipulated or controlled by neither priest nor church. Luther's emphasis was on the action of God in this

5 Bernard J. Cooke, *Christian Sacraments and Christian Personality* (N.Y.: Holt, Rinehart & Winston, 1965), p. 130.

sacrament, on the gift of grace, on receiving rather than doing. Moreover, he held that the Word of God and not the mass is the pivotal center of true worship. It is the preaching of the Word and not the sacrament that is the primary means of grace. It is never the sacrament by itself but always the sacrament conjoined with the Word that brings us the mercy and salvation of Christ.

Calvin like Luther had a doctrine of the real presence, but his concern was to show that it is the Spirit who makes Christ present to us. Unlike Luther he held to the localized presence of Jesus Christ in heaven, but he contended that we are lifted heavenward by the Spirit in the Communion service. He was very insistent that we encounter the whole Christ in this sacrament and not merely the spirit of Christ. "Christ does not simply present to us the benefit of His death and resurrection, but the very body in which He suffered and rose again."[6] His emphasis was on communication rather than commemoration. The sacrament is an instrument of the grace of God and not simply a sign of this grace. Calvin's views are reflected in the Geneva Catechism and the Scottish Confession.

Zwingli, the noted Reformer of Zurich, had a somewhat different interpretation of the sacrament. For Zwingli the sacrament is primarily a commemoration of Christ's sacrifice offered once for all on Calvary. It is also an occasion by which we pledge or reconsecrate ourselves to Christ. Zwingli maintained that we feed upon Christ spiritually in the supper by faith. Brian Gerrish calls Zwingli's position "symbolic memorialism" as over against the "symbolic instrumentalism" of Calvin.[7] In Zwingli's view the sacrament proclaims grace, but it does not give us grace. It is not so much a participation in Christ's sacrifice as a fellowship meal. Zwingli's position is mirrored in the Westminster Confession. It is also reflected in the theology of Karl Barth, although with certain modifications.

Heinrich Bullinger, Zwingli's successor in Zurich, sought to return to a more catholic understanding of the sacrament. Bullinger contended that in the sacrament we receive as well as remember. He conceived of two independent but parallel processes, a spiritual and a physical, in the holy supper. As we

---

6 John Calvin, *Commentary on the Epistles of Paul the Apostle to the Corinthians* 11:24, trans. John Pringle, Vol. I (Grand Rapids: Eerdmans reprint), p. 379.

7 See Brian A. Gerrish, "The Lord's Supper in the Reformed Confessions" in *Theology Today* (July, 1966), Vol. XXIII, No. 2, pp. 224-243.

eat and drink of the elements, at the same time the Holy Spirit implants within us the efficacy of Christ's atoning sacrifice. Gerrish calls this position "symbolic parallelism." Bullinger's views are represented in the Second Helvetic Confession and the Heidelberg Catechism.

All of the above positions contain some truth. But we hold that Calvin and Luther are closer to the real meaning of the sacrament than Zwingli. For the former, salvation is a present as well as a past event. The sacrament is not merely a proclamation of the grace of God but also a means of grace. The elements are symbols, but symbols which participate in the reality they represent. They are not merely outward signs but effectual signs. Through the Spirit they convey what they signify. Zwingli's major contribution is in conceiving of the sacrament as a fellowship meal and also an occasion for rededication to Christ. The recent Arnoldsheim Theses in Germany represent attempts on the continent to bring together Lutherans and Reformed in this vital area of theology.

## A REAPPRAISAL OF THIS SACRAMENT

In seeking to reformulate the theology of the Eucharist we must first understand that this sacrament was instituted for our salvation. Jesus associated the elements with His body and blood that was to be poured out for many for the forgiveness of sins (Mt. 26:26-29). He pointed to mystical communion with His body and blood as a precondition of salvation (Jn. 6:35f.).[8] Paul regarded the holy meal as a participation in the body and blood of Christ (I Cor. 10:16). Just as baptism sets us on the way to final salvation, so Communion keeps us on the way. As St. Ambrose stated so succinctly: "Because I always sin, I am always bound to take medicine." And the medicine of divine grace is given to us in no greater measure than in Holy Communion.

If we are to recover the full import of this sacrament we must view it as a proclamation and dramatization of the sacrifice of Christ on Calvary. But it must not be regarded as a repetition or extension of this sacrifice. Neither should it be seen as a continuation of the sacrifice, a term which Bernard Cooke sometimes uses. It can be considered a participation in

8 Jn. 6 continues to be a subject of theological controversy, but most New Testament scholars believe that the Eucharistic allusion is unmistakable. This must not be taken to imply that mystical communion with Christ is dependent on the sacrament.

the atoning sacrifice of Christ but not as an offering of this sacrifice.

The blessed sacrament should also be viewed as an occasion by which we present our sacrifices of praise and thanksgiving. The original meaning of eucharist *(eucharistia)* is thanksgiving. This is to say, we not only receive, but we also do. Our sacrifices are offered by Christ and united with His intercessions. But we do not offer Christ as our Roman Catholic and Anglo-Catholic brethren sometimes aver. We plead or appeal to His sacrifice as the sole ground of the acceptability of our self-offering. The Eucharist is "a showing forth, and a pleading before the Father, Christ's sacrifice once for all offered."[9] We can speak of a eucharistic sacrifice in the sense of a sacrifice of praise but not a propitiatory sacrifice (as Trent said). Moreover, we partake of the Lord's Supper not to gain merit, not to make ourselves worthy in God's sight but rather to give glory to God and to praise Him for the sacrifice of His Son on Calvary.

The time has come when we should again give serious consideration to the real presence of Jesus Christ in this holy sacrament. Indeed, we not only appropriate the fruits of His sacrifice, but we receive Jesus Christ Himself into our hearts. In each Communion Christ gives Himself to us anew. Yet one must be cautious when referring to His presence in the Eucharist. It is better to speak not of a physical or spiritual presence but of a sacramental presence of our Lord. This means that He makes Himself present in this sacrament in a way that is unique or incomparable. We must not affirm a materialized, localized presence of Christ but rather His personal presence via His Spirit and in the whole eucharistic action. It should be borne in mind that even Thomas Aquinas did not adhere to a localized presence; "substance" in his theology is nonspatial.

We affirm that in this sacrament the elements are laid hold of by the Holy Spirit and taken up in the body of Christ. The elements become channels of the real presence of Christ. Yet there is no transubstantiation; the elements are not changed into the substance of Christ. It is well to note that Paul refers to the Eucharistic host as bread (I Cor. 10:16, 17; 11:28). Nor do we uphold a view that has been denominated as parallelism. There are not two independent parallel processes but rather Christ, His body and blood, His power, are given in the reception of

---

[9] In *Plan of Church Union in North India and Pakistan,* 3rd revised ed. (Madras: Diocesan Press, 1957), p. 8.

the bread and wine and are indeed inseparable from these elements in the eucharistic rite.

In our view the relation between the divine and human in
Christ is paradigmatic for the relation between the spiritual
and material in this sacrament. Just as Christ was wholly man
as well as true God, so the elements are truly material as well
as spiritual. One might say that they are natural in composition
and supernatural in significance. The Roman Catholic view as
traditionally stated is docetic; the elements are only appearances
of the bread and wine.[10] The liberal (and also fundamentalist)
Protestant view verges towards the heresy of ebionitism; the
elements are only physical or outward signs of the spiritual
presence of Christ.

In line with many Roman Catholics today we hold that there
should be no adoration of the host or of the wine. Since the
elements have been consecrated to a holy use, they should be
respected but not worshiped. Roman Catholic and high Anglican churches are very insistent upon the reservation of the host,
and we have no objection to this so long as it is not maintained
that Christ is somehow localized in the bread. One should bear
in mind that it is not the bread as such but the eating of the
bread in faith that is the sacramental sign.[11]

This is not to deny that it is possible in one sense to speak
of a change in the elements insofar as Christ is present, for
where Christ is, everything is altered. Indeed, where Christ is,
everything is made to reflect His glory. But again it should be
stated that Christ is present in the whole action of the Eucharist. Just as pure water that is poured into an earthen vessel
will surely affect its interior (in that the vessel is now filled),
so divine grace that is given in bread and wine will certainly
have a marked effect upon these elements although not changing their physical composition. But it is well to remember

---

10 Some Catholic theologians are now insisting that the material reality of
the bread remains unchanged and are no longer referring to this reality as
simply an appearance or accident. Edward Schillebeeckx has stated: "The
physical reality does not change, otherwise there would no longer be any
eucharistic sign" ("Transubstantiation," *Worship*, Vol. 40, p. 337). And in
the words of Kilian McDonnell: "Only on condition that the materiality
of the bread remains can there be a eucharistic reality." In his *John Calvin,
The Church, and the Eucharist* (Princeton: Princeton University Press,
1967), p. 315.

11 That our views on this matter closely approximate those of Karl Rahner
can be seen in his essay "The Presence of Christ After Communion"
in his *Theological Investigations*, trans. Kevin Smyth (Baltimore: Helicon
Press, 1966), Vol. IV, pp. 312-320.

that it is not the elements so much as the hearts of believers that become the vessels of the Holy Spirit. The elements are only means to the goal which is the regeneration of persons. It should be noted that the traditional barriers between Roman Catholicism and Protestantism in this area are not as insuperable as might at first appear.

Again it should be reiterated that faith is absolutely necessary for the sacrament to be efficacious. The bread of life or the grace of our Lord Jesus Christ may very well be given to all, but only those who repent and believe benefit. Indeed, we are told that the sacrament will even have an adverse effect apart from faith (I Cor. 11:29, 30). Paul contends that some people actually become sick and die if they partake of the supper in an unworthy manner. Such persons do not meet Christ as their Savior but as their Judge.

It should be recognized that faith in this context means repentance and heartfelt trust in Christ. We do not have this kind of faith when we harbor grudges and hatreds against certain people. Jesus said that our gifts are not accepted at the altar until we are first reconciled with our neighbor (Mt. 5: 23, 24).

Faith also entails consecration and rededication. Zwingli is right that we must pledge ourselves to the service of Christ if the Lord's Supper is to be fully meaningful for us. For this reason the symbolism of going up to the altar is much more powerful than remaining in the pews for Communion. In many fundamentalist churches this dimension of Holy Communion has been lost sight of, and that is why the altar call in a service of revival has been found necessary.

As in the case of baptism we should be reminded that faith does not create the presence of Christ in the sacrament but instead acknowledges and receives this presence. The grace of God does not take root in our hearts unless we cling to Christ in faith; at the same time it is possible to be encountered by this grace without faith. But the seed then falls upon stony ground or among thorns rather than upon good soil (cf. Mt. 13:18-23).

Again we need to recover the truth that this holy supper is an eschatological banquet. It is an anticipation of our future glory, of the perfection which awaits us. It is a sign of the royal banquet in the kingdom of God when Jesus Christ Himself will eat and drink with us (cf. Mt. 26:29). Therefore it should be an occasion for joy and hope. Already we enter into fellowship with Christ and all the saints as we partake of this sacred meal; but our fellowship shall be consummated in a communion of perfect love in the kingdom of glory.

With our fathers in the faith (both Evangelical and Catholic) we hold that the sacrament does not communicate to us the salvation of Christ apart from the Word. The Word and the sacrament belong together, and although the former may exist apart from the latter, the latter can never be valid apart from the former. By the Word we understand both Christ's words of institution contained in Scripture and also the word of the sermon. The sacrament can be valid if the promises of Scripture are read and the words of Christ are given, but in order for it to be fully efficacious it must be grounded in the sermon.[12] Indeed, it is only when the Gospel is explicated to us that we are convicted of our sin and enabled to repent. Also it is only in the light of a sermon on the cross that we can properly discern the body in the sacrament. This is why there should be no private celebration of the sacrament except in extreme cases where one is too ill to participate in public worship. And even then one does not communicate in isolation but instead in the immediate presence of the pastor and elders and in the invisible company of the saints who are present through the mediation of the Spirit. That the word also needs the sacrament to be fully understood should be acknowledged as well. The word apart from the sacrament becomes a barren rationalism; the sacrament apart from the word degenerates into a magical ritualism. We concur in these remarks of Thomas à Kempis:

> Therefore hast Thou given me in my weakness Thy Sacred Body for the nourishment of my soul and body; and Thou hast set Thy Word as a lamp to my feet. Without these two I could not well live; for the Word of God is the light of my soul, and Thy Sacrament is the Bread of Life.[13]

It is important to consider the subject of the frequency of Communion. If Communion is indeed a spiritual medicine, as the church fathers sometimes described it, then Christians being

---

[12] One Catholic theologian contends: "The elements by themselves have no significance ... it is in the light of the word that we should understand the Lord's Supper. The word here has not primarily the function of consecrating and transforming, but of proclaiming and testifying." Hans Küng, *The Church*, trans. Ray and Rosaleen Ockenden (N.Y.: Sheed & Ward, 1967), p. 219.

[13] Thomas à Kempis, *Of the Imitation of Christ*, trans. Abbot Justin McCann (N.Y.: Mentor Books, 1957), Bk. IV, Ch. 11, p. 175.

yet sinners surely stand in need of it. The inner man cannot live apart from the bread of life, and this bread is given to us in the holy supper. The Reformers, Calvin and Luther, both recommended weekly Communion, although their churches never accepted the idea.[14] Today those who stand in the vanguard of the liturgical movement also advocate a weekly celebration of the supper.

Our view, however, is that the supper should not be celebrated *too* frequently, since then it might become commonplace, and also there should be careful preparation for the encounter with Christ in this sacrament. Father von Balthasar, the Jesuit writer, has rightly declared: "Sacramental reception of the Eucharist is vain, unless it is accompanied with living faith and love...."[15] The ideal to be sure is a weekly observance, but there are too many people in the kind of secularized society in which we live who are not yet ready for this. If repentance for sin is a precondition for valid Holy Communion, then perhaps a service of worship is necessary a week or several days prior to the celebration in order to lead people into repentance. One authority on worship has stated: "If repentance, reverence, and holy awe were Calvin's primary concern for the celebration of the Lord's Supper, these could easily be lost by instituting a weekly observance."[16] It is fallacious to argue that there cannot be authentic worship apart from the Eucharist. The Eucharist enriches worship, but it is the Spirit alone who fulfills the worship celebration. The Eucharist can be viewed as a culmination of the worship celebration, but the Word of God alone is the foundation for worship. It is well to remember the contention of the Reformers that it is not the omission of the sacrament that damns but the contempt of the sacrament. Our recommendation is for a monthly observance.

In the interest of church discipline we insist that there should be no indiscriminate communion. The holy supper is open to all who truly repent and believe, but it certainly should not be given to those who have no faith or those who lead lives of open scandal. The apostle warns against profaning the

---

14 It is interesting to note that the people in Geneva under Calvin complained that whereas previously as Catholics they were obligated to partake of Communion only once a year, now they were expected to partake at least four times a year.

15 Hans Urs von Balthasar, *Prayer*, trans. A. V. Littledale (Glen Rock, N.J.: Paulist Press), p. 96.

16 Frederick W. Schroeder, *Worship in the Reformed Tradition* (Philadelphia: United Church Press, 1966), p. 145.

body and blood of our Lord (I Cor. 11). Communion should
be reserved for the community of active believers, since it has
to do with the sanctification of the church and not the conversion of the world.

But although we oppose indiscriminate communion we certainly affirm the need for intercommunion. This is to say, the
sacrament should be open to baptized believers of all denominations. It should not be made conditional upon the level or
degree of one's understanding, because this would lead us into
Gnosticism, salvation by knowledge. One must acknowledge the
Lordship and Saviorhood of Christ, and His living presence in
this sacrament, but certainly there is no one correct idea of the
mode of His presence which should be the basis for participation. It is interesting to note that there is now intercommunion
between the Church of Denmark and the Church of Scotland,
and it is to be hoped that other Lutheran and Reformed
churches will also begin to share a common table and altar.
Intercommunion is also practiced in the Protestant community
of Taizé which includes Anglicans, Reformed and Lutheran.
This is not to deny that between some churches formidable
theological barriers remain, and these must somehow be sur-
mounted if intercommunion is to become generally accepted.

A word should perhaps be said concerning some of the new
experimental liturgies in which soft drinks and potato chips
(or something comparable) are substituted for the traditional
elements. Here we have to utter a word of admonition. We do
not depend upon soft drinks and potato chips for our sustenance
nor do they give proper nourishment; therefore they are not
adequate symbols of the heavenly food apart from which men
cannot live. Moreover, we hold that the words of Christ on this
matter must be taken literally, just as His words concerning
baptism and the preaching of the Gospel. Even as we cannot
substitute a modern devotional masterpiece for the Bible, so we
must be very careful in substituting any other food for the
fruit of the vine and bread.[17] This does not preclude the Christian community from having an Agape meal with other foods,
but the Agape meal or love feast was always distinguished from
the holy supper in the early church.[18]

---

[17] Under a papal dispensation rice wine has been used by Roman Catholics
in China in the Eucharistic rite. Our view is that if a change of this type
is necessitated by the cultural or historical situation, the church as a whole
must be moved by the Holy Spirit to make the innovation.

[18] In the New Testament it seems that Communion was sometimes celebrated in conjunction with the love feast, but the two were definitely sep-

In our view there can be no complete Christian renewal until the holy supper again becomes the bond of unity for all Christians. It is scandalous that at meetings of the World Council of Churches separate Communion services are held in order to meet the requirements of various denominations. The Evangelical mass and the Catholic mass should be viewed as correlative. The Communion table and the altar both symbolize aspects of the Christian faith which need to be preserved. Holy Communion is a fellowship meal as well as a eucharistic sacrifice, and unless we hold onto both truths we fall either into secularization or magic.

Holy Communion should again become the medium of reconciliation in the church, and yet this does not predicate liturgical uniformity. So long as the sacrament is given in the context of the Word, it is not unduly important whether the priest or pastor stands behind or in front of the table-altar or whether the people come forward or remain seated. There should be a variety of sacramental liturgies, but there is need for a basic unity in faith and love. Christians should learn to love one another as brothers and sisters; they need also to share a basic understanding of the meaning of the sacrifice of Christ which is symbolized and made present for our salvation in the rite of Holy Communion. It is to be hoped that what is now the principal barrier to Christian unity may become the key to the reunion of all Christians under the lordship of Christ.

arated by the end of the second century. See M. H. Shepherd, Jr., "The Agape" in *The Interpreter's Dictionary of the Bible*, Vol. I (N.Y.: Abingdon Press, 1962), pp. 53, 54. See also Neville Clark, "Agape and Eucharist" in his *An Approach to the Theology of the Sacraments* (Chicago: Alec R. Allenson, 1956), pp. 49-59.

# FIVE

# EVANGELICAL CONFESSION

## THE NEED FOR CONFESSION

Our age has been characterized as one of despair and meaninglessness. According to Martin Marty modern man is afflicted both with *anomie* (rootlessness) and *accidie* (boredom) .[1] Tillich has asserted that the anxiety of meaninglessness is the chief malady today. And behind meaninglessness is the anxiety of guilt, the consciousness that one is alienated from the ground and source of his being. Indeed, does not man seek to stifle the voice of his conscience by immersing himself in trivialities and penultimate concerns, and does he not in this way become inwardly empty and distraught? No man can live a full life without being committed to the eternal God, but such commitment is impossible without a recognition of one's guilt and inner lostness.

It cannot be denied that there is a rising incidence of mental illness in modern technicalized culture. Closely related to this is the alarming increase in suicide and various forms of addiction. Behind much of the mental and spiritual illness of today is the problem of personal guilt. O. Hobart Mowrer, a Christian psychologist, maintains that modern Protestantism has not been able to deal with this problem.[2] Pastoral psychology is not the breakthrough that many had hoped it would be. Even ministers seem unable to cope with their feelings of guilt, and perhaps this is one reason why many of the clergy are included among the patients in our mental hospitals.

A growing number of Protestant theologians today are pointing to the need for private, auricular confession. We need only mention in this connection Dietrich Bonhoeffer, George MacLeod, Martin Marty, Eduard Thurneysen, Max Thurian and

[1] Martin Marty, *Varieties of Unbelief* (N.Y.: Holt, Rinehart & Winston, 1964), pp. 103f.

[2] See his *The Crisis in Psychiatry and Religion* (Princeton, N.J.: Van Nostrand, 1961) and *The New Group Therapy* (Princeton: Van Nostrand, 1964).

William Stringfellow. Bonhoeffer states the case for evangelical confession in his well-known book *Life Together*. Among those in the world of psychiatry and psychology who are contending for the restoration of confession within Protestantism are Paul Tournier, Theodore Bovet, Bernard Martin and O. Hobart Mowrer. Mowrer advocates shared group confession rather than private confession in the presence of a pastor or priest.

Many Protestant churches seek to meet the problem of personal guilt by a public prayer of confession. Yet what this prayer usually deals with is sin in general, and the particular sins of the parishioners are overlooked. Too often the emphasis in Protestant theology has been on the general sinfulness of man rather than on specific sins. It is true that no area of man's life is free from the corruption of sin and therefore exempt from the need of forgiveness. Yet we should also recognize that the truly biblical way of acknowledging our sinful state is by the confession of particular sins which are the fruit and expression of this state. As Georgia Harkness has observed: "A general confession is good, but in it lurks the danger of 'acknowledging and bewailing' humanity's sins and not our own."[3] Moreover, a public prayer of confession particularly when accompanied by a declaration of pardon or absolution can give one the impression that forgiveness is automatic. It thereby becomes a means of easy salvation. This is not to deny that a public prayer of confession when rightly formulated and when followed by a declaration of pardon that is addressed specifically to those who are truly repentant can bring consolation to many disturbed people. Yet what is called for is something more: those who remain stricken with guilt after the general prayer of confession should be given an opportunity to unburden themselves more concretely and to hear the Scriptural words of forgiveness addressed to them personally.

The rise of psychotherapy and psychoanalysis in modern Western society is due partly to the inability of our churches to cope with the problem of guilt. Modern psychotherapy can even be viewed as a secularized form of confession (Thurneysen). The popularity of counseling courses in our seminaries and the marked increase in counseling services in many churches testifies to the vacuum created by the demise of confession. Much of what goes under the name of pastoral counseling is in

---

3 Georgia Harkness, *Religious Living* (N.Y.: Hazen Books on Religion, Association Press, 1937), p. 39.

reality an attempt to adapt secular psychotherapy to a churchly environment. Sebastian de Grazia has aptly remarked that the psychoanalyst has taken the place of the Father Confessor for modern man.[4] William Cole maintains that the secular psychotherapist has become the spiritual mentor of many Protestants.

Secular counseling has helped countless numbers of people, but it does not give absolution. It can bring comfort and guidance to people but not the assurance of the forgiveness of sins. It can contribute to the rehabilitation of men but not to their justification. In O. Hobart Mowrer's opinion psychoanalysis has become a means of cheap grace. Because of the exorbitant fees of many analysts and counselors, it can even be viewed as a method of buying one's salvation.

Martin Marty avers that the great need in Protestantism today is to restore the office of confession.

> The restoration of confession to the evangelical churches — as both a public and a private act — will be the test of the seriousness of the hidden discipline. With surprising suddenness we have discovered — almost too late — that the neglect of confession has meant a relapse in the modern world of Christians into two false ways: legalism and relaxation. Under the quiet roofs, along the broad, tree-lined avenues of our villages, in the glass and steel of our apartments, on our farms, live people who use gentility to cover up terror. They use politeness to cover up loneliness; apathy to cover up despair; escape to cover up the vacuum that will not let us be alone with ourselves. In the face of this condition, people of other professions who deal with persons ask the evangelical churches why they have given up their greatest disciplinary and therapeutic treasure, confession of sins and absolution.[5]

William Stringfellow after discussing the indispensable role of confession in public worship and pastoral care goes on to declare:

> Yet confession hardly survives in contemporary Protestantism. Improvisations have been introduced more or less in the place of confession, some of them concocted in the seminaries which each year discharge men for the ordained ministry who are amateur, part-time therapists or who have been enough indoctrinated in group dynamics to fancy their skill in human manipulation, or who earnestly intend to "work with people in solving their problems." No discount is made here for the significance of psychiatry and psychology, but these skills will not be acquired in the seminaries. And no one who has been in politics, as I have, would minimize the importance of what is lately called

---

4 See his *Errors of Psychotherapy* (Garden City, N.Y.: Doubleday, Inc., 1952).
5 Martin Marty, *The Hidden Discipline* (St. Louis: Concordia, 1962), p. 95.

"group dynamics", but neither is this a substitute in the Church for confession and absolution and intercession.[6]

Roman Catholics also are in a quandary over this matter. The Roman church has an elaborate system of penitential discipline including confession and absolution; yet studies indicate that the number of Catholics in mental hospitals in this country is as high as it is for Protestants, if not higher. Some critics contend that by making confession into a law requiring the confession of every sin, the Catholic church has promoted scrupulosity. James Kavanaugh voices this complaint: "Our confessional becomes a travesty when we compare it to the Christian vision of pardon. Christ promised freedom and we offer imprisonment and guilt. Christ spoke of joy and we offer only a break in tension to be followed by a more painful relapse."[7] In the view of Father Joseph Nolan: "Our ministry of penance is in vast need of restructuring, and yet its formulation has a low priority everywhere, not just in Rome. . . . In the past we have often multiplied sins and burdened consciences. The future holds the possibility of fewer but better confessions."[8] Nolan is among those Roman Catholic scholars who are now advocating both a freer form of private confession and a public prayer of confession. Louis Monden has given a penetrating reappraisal of sin and confession in Catholic theology in his *Sin, Liberty and Law*.[9] He maintains that the penitent should focus his attention not on his own sins so much as on Christ's welcoming love. He also advocates the restoration of a collective liturgical celebration of confession. Significantly he desires that confession and spiritual direction be "carefully kept apart" from psychological counseling. In some avant garde Roman Catholic circles "lay confession" is being advocated in addition to "sacramental confession."[10]

Dutch Catholicism has particularly been open to changes in the rite of confession. In April of 1969 the Dutch Pastoral Council called for the development of new forms of penance;

---

6 William Stringfellow, *A Private and Public Faith* (Grand Rapids: Eerdmans, 1962), p. 50.

7 James Kavanaugh, *A Modern Priest Looks at His Church* (N.Y.: Trident, 1967), p. 87. Since the publication of this book Kavanaugh has resigned from the priesthood.

8 Joseph T. Nolan, "General Absolution: The Need For It, The Case For It" in *The National Catholic Reporter*, Vol. 4, No. 13 (Jan. 24, 1968), p. 8.

9 Louis Monden, *Sin, Liberty and Law*, trans. Joseph Donceel (N.Y.: Sheed & Ward, 1965).

10 See Walter Kasper, "Confession Outside the Confessional" in Hans Küng, ed., *The Sacraments: An Ecumenical Dilemma* (Glen Rock, N.J.: Paulist Press, 1967), pp. 31-42.

it urged that the sacrament regain "its original community character" and be "freed from the oppressiveness of the confessional."[11] In several Dutch churches today members of the congregation publicly recite a statement of contrition and receive absolution in a group from the priest although private confession is still available for those who desire it.

O. Hobart Mowrer contends that many priests in their attempt to come to terms with Freudianism are viewing neurosis as sickness rather than guilt, and thereby the anxiety of guilt is not really overcome. His position is that a neurosis "is nothing but a state of guilt that has been neither admitted nor atoned for, and the notion that a person needs some special kind of professional treatment to deliver him from such a condition is surely one of the great illusions of modern times."[12]

## CONFESSION IN THEOLOGICAL HISTORY

To understand the disappearance of confession in Protestant Christianity, one must be acquainted with the protest of the Reformers against the Catholic sacrament of penance and also with the development of this particular sacrament in the history of the church prior to the Reformation. It should be noted that in the early church the dominant practice was public confession of sins and a public act of reconciliation with the congregation. Due partly to the influence of Celtic monasticism, private auricular confession of sins became popular, although spiritually gifted laymen as well as priests were chosen as confessors. In Eastern Orthodox Christianity people who desired to unburden themselves generally went not to the priests but to those who had a special charism and were considered holy men (usually monks).

It was not until the thirteenth century that penance became an official sacrament in the Roman Catholic church. The recitation of sins was now made into a law, and it was required that every Christian make his confession to the clergy. In Catholic theology the sacrament of penance is divided into contrition, confession and satisfaction. Satisfaction signifies a penance imposed by the church upon the penitent which partly expiates not only the guilt of the sin but also the temporal punishment which remains due to sin after the guilt has been forgiven. The principal kinds of penances that have been imposed are alms giving, fasting and prayer. In late medieval

---

[11] See *National Catholic Reporter* (April 23, 1969), Vol. 5, No. 6, p. 9.
[12] O. Hobart Mowrer, *The New Group Therapy*, p. 225.

theology the penitential system became closely tied to the practice of indulgences, which are remissions of penalty due for confessed sins granted by the church. When these indulgences were made available on the basis of financial contributions to the church, the penitential system was shaken to its foundations. The whole idea of indulgences is now being carefully reappraised by Catholic ecumenists.[13]

It is against this background that we should try to understand the criticisms which the Reformers leveled against the sacrament of penance. In general it can be said that they saw it as a kind of works righteousness by which people sought to gain satisfaction for sin by means of certain penances. They also held that it detracted from baptism, since it was seen as a second plank in our salvation. According to Luther if we sin after baptism we do not need a new sacrament; instead we should simply return to our baptism and recover the grace that has been given to us once for all. The Reformers also objected to the fact that confession was obligatory or compulsory. In this same connection they deplored the requirement for the meticulous recitation of every sin. It should be noted that the Council of Trent reaffirmed without equivocation the necessity for confession through the spoken word of all mortal sins.

Yet it would be a mistake to suppose that the Protestant Reformers wished to throw out private confession. Luther even retained confession or penance as a third sacrament throughout much of his career, although he drastically reinterpreted it to bring it into line with evangelical principles. The Augsburg Confession sought to maintain both confession and private absolution for the church. The Apology of the Augsburg Confession even calls repentance a sacrament (Ch. 7, Art. 3). Calvin also made a place for sacramental confession, but he did not view it as a sacrament. Like Luther and Melanchthon he understood it as a means of grace but not as an atonement for sin. It is a means of obtaining the assurance of pardon and strengthening our will to service. In Calvin's view it should be regarded as a form of pastoral care and also of church discipline. He believed that it could prepare one for Holy Communion, and

---

13 See Gregory Baum, "Silence on Indulgences" in *The Ecumenist* (March/ April, 1965), Vol. 3, No. 3, pp. 37-39; Karl Rahner, "Remarks on the Theology of Indulgences" in his *Theological Investigations*, Vol. II, trans. Karl H. Kruger (London: Darton, Longman & Todd, 1963), pp. 175-201; and Christian Duquoc, "Notes on Indulgences" in Carra de Vaux Saint-Cyr, et al., *The Sacrament of Penance* (Glen Rock, N.J.: Paulist Press, 1966), pp. 74-78.

therefore he encouraged its use. The appropriate person to hear the confession, he said, is the pastor. The Second Helvetic Confession also allows for private confession in the presence of the pastor or a Christian brother (Ch. XIV).

Confession lingered on for a century and a half in the churches of the Reformation. In the Scottish Presbyterian church offenders were required to make a public confession of sin before the elders and the congregation. In the Methodist class meetings inaugurated by John Wesley a free form of confession flourished for a time. Wesley also advocated private confession to a spiritual guide. Yet by the nineteenth century the practice of auricular confession had practically disappeared in Protestantism. There were efforts on the part of such men as John Nevin, Wilhelm Loehe and Nathan Pusey to restore the office of confession, but these efforts did not bear lasting fruit except in some high church circles. Confession and absolution were revived in the ministry of Johann Christoph Blumhardt, but the evangelical churches for the most part closed their eyes to the benefits of such rites.

One is prompted to inquire into the causes of the loss of confession within Protestantism particularly in light of the fact that it was strongly advocated by the Reformers. Certainly the Enlightenment should be given serious consideration in this connection, since it affected both orthodox and liberal Protestantism. In the philosophy of the Enlightenment sin consists essentially in ignorance and weakness; one needs only to be enlightened and he will then act according to the truth. Needless to say, this type of thinking undercuts the urgency of the confession of sins, since what is deemed necessary is no longer forgiveness but knowledge. Evangelical Pietism also hastened the demise of confession. Both Spener and Francke protested against automatic absolution and compulsory confession, which had reappeared in German Lutheranism.[14] In addition the fact that many pastors were charging fees for hearing confessions served to place this rite under a cloud. The modern emphasis upon the free individual, which was particularly evident in the nineteenth century, also militated against confession, since it was considered demeaning to make oneself dependent upon the church or any other person in this way. Fichte contended that the human soul stands in need of no external mediators, since it carries the divine spark within itself. William Henley

---

[14] Spener nevertheless believed that every Christian should have some spiritual confidant with whom he could share his burdens.

voiced the prevailing mood when he said that man is master of his own fate and captain of his own soul. The ever-recurring tide of anti-Romanism in post-Reformation Protestantism has also cast a shadow over confession, since anything that remotely smacks of Catholicism is suspect.

Probably the principal factor in the demise of confession has been the loss of sin-consciousness in the modern age. The churches, particularly the main-line Protestant churches, have assumed a lamentably bourgeois character. The bourgeois church views itself as a society of respectable, law-abiding people. The transgressions of its people are seen as faults and misdemeanors but not sins. That man is basically wicked and perverse is simply no longer believed by most moderns. Bonhoeffer has very well described the situation:

> The pious fellowship permits no one to be a sinner. So everybody must conceal his sin from himself and from the fellowship. We dare not to be sinners. Many Christians are unthinkably horrified when a real sinner is suddenly discovered among the righteous. So we remain in our sin, living in lies and hypocrisy.[15]

### A REAPPRAISAL OF CONFESSION

It is our contention that confession needs to be restored to our churches, but it must be of an evangelical character. It must be solidly anchored in the biblical witness to the free grace of God and should be in accord with the basic recommendations of the Protestant Reformers.

The biblical basis for confession and absolution essentially rests upon such passages as Mt. 16:19; 18:15-18; and Jn. 20:23. The latter is particularly significant: "If you forgive the sins of any, they are forgiven; if you retain the sins of any, they are retained." Most commentators agree that Jesus gave to His disciples the authority to declare the forgiveness of sins in His name. In the evangelical understanding the words of absolution do not create forgiveness; rather they convey the assurance of a forgiveness already given by Jesus Christ. It is interesting to note that in Jn. 20:23 we have the perfect tense given in the Greek — "they have been forgiven" and "they have been retained."

In making an evangelical case for confession we also appeal to the biblical insight that the Christian can be a means of grace to his neighbor. As Jesus said: "He who hears you hears

15 Dietrich Bonhoeffer, *Life Together*, trans. John Doberstein (N.Y.: Harper & Row, 1954), p. 110.

me" (Lk. 10:16; cf. Mk. 13:11). And Paul declared that "it pleased God through the folly of what we preach to save those who believe" (I Cor. 1:21; cf. II Cor. 5:20). We might also appeal to Jms. 5:16 in which we are told to confess our sins to one another. Or we can point to the Old Testament passage II Sam. 12:1-14. After David repents of his sin, the prophet Nathan declares: "The Lord also has put away your sin."

By evangelical confession we understand the confession of sins in the presence of a pastor or Christian brother and the receiving of the assurance of pardon based on the promises in Scripture. Evangelical confession should not be seen as meritorious; it is a recognition of our unworthiness rather than an attempt to make ourselves worthy in the sight of God. It also is not to be viewed as a means of gaining satisfaction for sin. Satisfaction has been procured by Jesus Christ once for all, and what is needed is to acknowledge this salvation. Confession is not the prerequisite for obtaining forgiveness but rather for hearing the word of forgiveness. Again we contend that confession should not be made into a rule. It should proceed from the depths of the heart and not under external compulsion. We also hold that private auricular confession should not be seen as necessary for salvation. One may go to God directly, and for many people this is sufficient. Confession is simply a crutch or aid to many of those who are weak in faith and who need to hear the Scriptural promises addressed to them personally from the mouth of a Christian brother.

Bonhoeffer reminds us that we may be deceiving ourselves by avoiding private confession.[16] We may be confessing only to ourselves and granting ourselves forgiveness. Confession in the presence of a brother gives us the opportunity to bare our soul in a concrete way before Christ who speaks to us through our brother. Yet we cannot argue that because God has bound Himself to His Word and Spirit we therefore cannot go to Him directly with our troubles. Since we hear His Word in Scripture and the sermon and because His Spirit dwells within us, private confession and absolution are not to be regarded as mandatory.[17]

Concerning absolution we hold that this is given not by the confessor but rather by Jesus Christ Himself. It is conveyed through the word of the Gospel which should be stated by the confessor, and in this way he himself becomes instrumental in

---

[16] Dietrich Bonhoeffer, *Life Together*, pp. 115, 116.

[17] Confession becomes mandatory when we have wronged one of our brethren; then we must go to him directly and be reconciled (Mt. 5:24).

the restoration and consolation of the sinner. Yet because it is
God alone who forgives, the formula that should be used in
the confessional situation is not *"absolvo te"* ("I absolve you")
but rather "I assure you that your sins are forgiven" or "Christ
has absolved you" or something similar.

One feature that is indispensable to confession as well as to
the Catholic sacrament of penance is the rule of absolute secrecy.
One will not feel free to unburden himself in the presence of
others unless he knows with certainty that they will hold what he
says in confidence. Luther held to the inviolability of the seal
of confession. Confession, he says in his *Table Talk,* "is made not
to me but to Christ: since He keeps it secret I keep it secret."

Evangelical confession should be seen as a form of pastoral
care. Whether it should be considered a sacrament is an open
question since there are no visible signs employed, but it certainly can be viewed as sacramental. It is a practical means of
gaining a deeper assurance of God's mercy and forgiveness. It
also serves to prepare one for Holy Communion.

Thurneysen has rightly contended that there can be no
evangelical confession apart from admonition.[18] The pastoral
advisor should not only assure his hearers of God's forgiveness
but also point them to God's law. He should inform them that
they are now under an obligation to break with the sin to which
they have yielded and consecrate themselves anew to the will
of God. He should also remind them that they now have the
power to obey through the gift of the Spirit of God. Jesus said
to the paralytic who was healed: "Sin no more, that nothing
worse befall you" (Jn. 5:14), and those who represent Christ
must give similar words of admonition.

There may even be a place for acts of penance in a rite of
evangelical confession. Yet these should not be seen as acts of
reparation but rather as tokens of gratefulness for the victory
over sin won by Christ. Penances that are suggested by the
pastor-confessor should be regarded not as penalties for sin but
rather as disciplines which enable us to overcome sin in our own
lives. They should be treated more as efforts at reformation
rather than as means of satisfaction for sin.

Just as evangelical confession should be distinguished from
the Catholic sacrament of penance so it must also not be con-

---

18 See Eduard Thurneysen, "Evangelical Confession" in Walter Luthi and
Eduard Thurneysen, *Preaching-Confession-The Lord's Supper,* trans. Francis
Broske (Richmond: John Knox Press, 1960); and Eduard Thurneysen, *A
Theology of Pastoral Care,* trans. Jack Worthington and Thomas Wieser
(Richmond: John Knox, 1962), pp. 310f.

fused with psychological counseling. Whereas confession concerns man's standing in the sight of God, counseling has to do
primarily with man's relationship to his fellowman. In the
counseling relationship the aim is to bring about catharsis and
rehabilitation. The goal in confession is to assure the sinner of
God's forgiveness, of the justification procured by Christ. The
appeal in counseling is directed to man's innate recuperative
powers. In the words of one astute observer: "The analytic
method is dependent on the help one finds in medicine and
oneself."[19] The appeal in confession, on the other hand, is to
the word of the cross, the promise of forgiveness declared in
Scripture. This is not to deny that counseling, even the most
radical form of non-directive counseling, has been of immense
aid to many people. Yet man stands in need of more than self-
understanding and of integration with his cultural environment.
He will still be troubled by guilt unless he has the experience
of Christ's salvation and the assurance that his sins are forgiven.
As Victor Frankl maintains, the prime need of man is not self-
fulfillment but self-transcendence. The deepest yearning of man
is to lose himself in a cause or power higher than himself. And
for Christians this cause can only be the kingdom of God, and
this higher reality can be none other than Jesus Christ.

We have been speaking here mainly of counseling as this is
understood in secular psychotherapy, but much of what we have
said also applies to pastoral counseling. As Mowrer has reminded
us, "pastoral counseling has been largely inspired by and
patterned upon secular psychotherapy."[20] Thurneysen maintains
that much that goes on under the name of pastoral care is in
reality psychological counsel in religious garb.[21] According to
Seward Hiltner pastoral counseling and the truly effective
counseling that is done in the secular world have essentially
the same basic attitude, method and approach.[22] Some men in
the field of pastoral counseling, such as William Hulme, have
sought to ground their discipline more solidly in biblical

---

19 Kurt Koch, *Seelsorge und Okkultismus* (Reith - Wustenroth, 1953), p.
278. For the English translation see his *Christian Counseling and Occultism*,
trans. Andrew Petter (Grand Rapids: Kregel, 1965).

20 O. Hobart Mowrer, *The Crisis in Psychiatry and Religion*, p. 107.

21 Eduard Thurneysen, *A Theology of Pastoral Care*, p. 214.

22 Seward Hiltner, *The Counselor in Counseling* (Nashville: Abingdon-
Cokesbury Press, 1952), p. 11. Hiltner's dependence upon secular psychotherapy can be seen in his remark: "The pastor does not coerce . . . or direct.
Instead he attempts to lead out or draw out resources and strengths which
can become operative only as they are helped to well up within the parish-
ioner" (p. 10).

theology, but it is well for purposes of clarification to make a distinction between counseling, including pastoral counseling, and confession.

That kind of counseling which entails giving men spiritual guidance and leading them into prayer might better be called spiritual direction. This term is deeply rooted in the tradition of the church, and it is much more theologically appropriate than the term counseling. Yet even spiritual direction is not absolution. In absolution the pastor-confessor communicates God's forgiveness and does not merely direct the penitent to God's mercy.

We hold that confession can be made to any Christian brother. Luther declared: "When I am troubled and sad, distressed and discouraged . . . if then my neighbor or brother comes to me, I should unburden myself to him in the assurance that his word of comfort has God's 'yes' in heaven."[23] Is not this the essence of the Reformation doctrine of the priesthood of believers — to be priests to one another?

This is not to assert that any Christian can be a spiritual director and confessor. It requires a special charism or various kinds of charisms. Surely one of these is prayerful listening; another may well be the discerning of spirits, and still another spiritual wisdom. The pastor who supposedly is endowed with some spiritual gifts in line with his calling is probably the logical person for this office. We should rethink the pastoral image, which is now very obscure in the minds of many people. Hans Küng contends that Protestantism needs to upgrade its office of the ministry. In our judgment the minister should be seen as a shepherd and priest rather than an administrator, a social reformer, a public relations man or a defender of public morality. He should also be regarded as a man of piety and biblical wisdom. Too often, however, the pastor is seen as a judge and moral censor, and this is why many people with deep-seated problems find him unapproachable.

The pastor should again be thought of as the father of a spiritual family and the shepherd of a definite flock, but we must take care not to elevate him unduly. We must beware of the peril of sacerdotalism in which the pastor is viewed as a special mediator between God and men. The shepherd should be recognized as a fellow-sinner, one who also stands in need of God's forgiveness.

---

23 Roland Bainton, ed. and trans., *Luther's Meditations on the Gospels* (Philadelphia: Westminster, 1957), p. 87.

Our suggestion is that the church give serious consideration to the office of a visiting confessor. Such a person might very well be a trained layman endowed with certain spiritual gifts. His task would be to visit one church after another for the sole purpose of hearing confessions and pronouncing absolution. The reason for this suggestion is that our people are not sufficiently acquainted with the special priestly role of the ordained ministry, and also many ministers have not yet been educated to see themselves in this role. Again, many lay people would be reluctant to confess their sins in the presence of a pastor, since Protestant pastors are notorious for not keeping confidences. Perhaps what is needed is a formal pledge of secrecy from the pastors at their ordination and also from laymen who might be designated as confessors.

Confession should also be encouraged in prayer fellowships. The early Methodists in their class meetings practiced mutual confession and edification. Mowrer is very much in favor of shared group confession. The Oxford Group of Frank Buchman in this century has pioneered in this practice and has been commended by such theologians as Emil Brunner and Dietrich Bonhoeffer. Alcoholics Anonymous also has shared confession coupled with restitution, and has found it to be very salutary.

The kind of group therapy advocated by Mowrer and also that exemplified in the Oxford Group movement are not beyond criticism. One danger is the temptation to exhibitionism — the more gory the sins, the more thrilling it is to the group. Another objection is that no word of assurance of pardon is given. The confession itself is regarded as therapeutic. But this again is to place confession on the psychological level and to make no room for the miracle of divine forgiveness.[24] The Salvation Army and certain Pentecostal groups are closer to the biblical position in their penitent's bench and prayer room where the penitent receives the assurance of pardon from Christian workers.

In Reformed Protestantism a distinction has traditionally been drawn between a sin against an individual and a sin against the community. If one sins against another person without doing obvious harm to the community in which he lives and works, then he need not confess that sin publicly; rather

---

[24] In Mowrer's philosophy in particular mutual confession and acceptance loom much more important than the divine word of forgiveness. According to him guilt is the fear of being found out by the significant others in one's life rather than a state of alienation between man and God.

he should go to his brother against whom he sinned and unburden himself (cf. Mt. 5:24). He may also go to his pastor or another Christian brother particularly if the party whom he has wronged did not grant him forgiveness. On the other hand if his sin has become a public scandal or if it has brought reproach upon his family and community, then he should probably make a public confession as well.

The church today needs to do much experimentation in this area, for it must be recognized that some kind of confession is sorely needed. Bonhoeffer has declared: "It is . . . only by redis-covering the divine office of confession that the Protestant Church can find its way back to a concrete ethic such as it possessed at the time of the Reformation."[25] In this anxiety-ridden age people need to be given a concrete opportunity to disclose their sins to a Christian brother and then to receive the same kind of comfort which the paralytic heard from the lips of Jesus: "Take heart, my son; your sins are forgiven" (Mt. 9:2).

---

25 Dietrich Bonhoeffer, *Ethics*, trans. Eberhard Bethge (N.Y.: Macmillan, 1949), pp. 292, 293.

# SIX

# CHURCH DISCIPLINE

## BREAKDOWN OF CHURCH DISCIPLINE

One of the causes of the dearth of spiritual vitality in the church today is the breakdown of church discipline. In the past few decades there has been a steady lowering of standards for church membership, both doctrinal and moral. Many churches under social and ecclesiastical pressures to increase their membership have practically abandoned membership standards. Franklin Littell tells of a single Methodist church in Atlanta that took in 462 individuals on one Sunday morning without even the minimum instruction and guidance.[1] Yet our churches are not retaining the members that they receive on a mass scale. Church attendance, Sunday School enrollment, applications for mission work, and the number of students for the ministry are all in decline in the mainline churches in America. Emil Brunner's words are very much to the point: "Count among Church members such as openly do not confess Christ, and the Church can no longer be considered a community of believers, but only as an institution, an instrument for the development of the believing community."[2]

The signs of the breakdown of church discipline are numerous. First we can point to the practice of indiscriminate communion. This means that the table of the Lord is made available to all persons regardless of their beliefs or manner of life. It should be noted that America's great theologian, Jonathan Edwards, was compelled to resign from one of his churches because he resisted community pressures for open communion. Another earmark of the disappearance of church discipline is the scandal of infant baptism. It appears that the great majority of children who are brought to the church are baptized irrespective of the beliefs of their parents or godparents. The state

---

[1] Kyle Haselden and Martin Marty, eds., *What's Ahead For the Churches?* (N.Y.: Sheed & Ward, 1964), p. 83.

[2] Emil Brunner, *The Divine-Human Encounter,* trans. Amandus W. Loos (Philadelphia: Westminster, 1943), p. 185.

churches in Europe are in more trouble in this area than are
the American churches, but standards are falling in this country
also. The lack of catechetical training surely is another evidence
of the sad state of our disciplinary procedures. While in former
years many churches, particularly those of Reformed and Lutheran background, had intensive catechetical instruction for
their young people, this is now largely a thing of the past. Confirmation classes are very much in vogue among the mainline
Protestant churches, but what the students are taught is usually
not the biblical message or the substance of the faith but rather
the history and polity of their own denominations. Such classes
are often arranged for a period of only a few weeks, whereas the
older catechetical classes sometimes lasted for as long as two
years. It is a sad commentary upon contemporary Protestantism
that the great majority of our young people who are being
received into membership are biblically illiterate, despite their
Sunday School training. Finally we should mention the notable
decrease in heresy trials in modern Protestantism. Some observers
hold that this is a favorable omen, since it indicates a growing
respect among our people for differences in opinion. But it
may just as well represent a false tolerance which treats doctrinal
matters lightly. Too many Christians today abide by the
spurious attitude that it doesn't matter what one believes so
long as he is sincere.

There is much talk today of taking the church into the world,
but we need also to warn of the encroachment of the world into
the church. The small sects and renewal movements are right
in their protest against the creeping secularization of our
churches. Instead of Christian stewardship too many of our
churches rely upon bazaars, dinners and bingo to meet their
financial obligations. In order to attract young people some of
our churches, particularly in the suburbs, sponsor dances. This
author has known of dances that were held even for junior high
school children, which certainly signifies a capitulation to the
spirit of the culture. What is needed in this era of the population
explosion is a protest against the trend towards early dating and
marriage. For young adults, some of the more sophisticated
parishes have instituted bars in the church basement or parish
hall. Despite much lip service given to the ideal of racial brotherhood, our churches are still for the most part segregated on the
basis of race and class. H. Richard Niebuhr's trenchant observation that the sources of our denominations are social rather than
theological or doctrinal still holds true today. Finally a word

should be said about the growing worldliness of our clergy. Every minister is worthy of his hire, but even students newly out of seminary are now demanding salaries that greatly exceed those of the laborers in their congregations. Even the more conservative ministers are seeking the very best that the world has to offer in the way of material goods. Our Reformed fathers upheld the ideal of a dignified simplicity, but this ideal seems to have fallen by the wayside.

Whereas once it was possible to speak of a Christian style of life, this is no longer meaningful for most church people. Yet we can speak of a Moslem style of life or a Communist style of life. The reason is that Islam and Communism represent disciplined communities, while discipline is no longer in effect in most of our churches. It must be recognized that a re-action is setting in among many serious Christians. Voices are beginning to clamor for the restoration of church discipline. Yet it is immensely difficult to go against the Establishment on this issue, since the churches are geared to big membership and big budgets. It is interesting to note that the General Conference of the Methodist Church (in Denver in 1962) explicitly forbade the removal of dead wood from membership rolls, despite the protestations of those who were seeking reform on this matter.

## THE BIBLICAL BASIS FOR CHURCH DISCIPLINE

Church discipline is based primarily upon the words of Jesus concerning the keys of the kingdom: "I will give you the keys of the kingdom of heaven, and whatever you bind on earth shall be bound in heaven, and whatever you loose on earth shall be loosed in heaven" (Mt. 16:19; cf. Jn. 20:23). The Heidelberg Catechism contends that this statement refers to both the preaching of the Word and church discipline (Q. 83). That the Christian community is obligated to reprove and discipline its members is explicitly affirmed by our Lord:

> If your brother sins against you, go and tell him his fault, between you and him alone. If he listens to you, you have gained your brother. But if he does not listen, take one or two others along with you, that every word may be confirmed by the evidence of two or three witnesses. If he refuses to listen to them, tell it to the church; and if he refuses to listen even to the church, let him be to you as a Gentile and a tax collector. Truly, I say to you, whatever you bind on earth shall be bound in heaven, and whatever you loose on earth shall be loosed in heaven (Mt. 18:15-18)

Those who champion an inclusive church membership often

point in defense of their views to Jesus' admonition against
judging (Mt. 7:1-5). But a closer examination of His statement
reveals that He did not prohibit all judging but only that which
is characterized by hypocrisy. As He said: "You hypocrite, first
take the log out of your own eye, and then you will see clearly
to take the speck out of your brother's eye." In a similar vein
He declared: "Do not judge by appearances, but judge with
right judgment" (Jn. 7:24).

The apostle Paul also expatiates on the problem of judging.
In his view the church should take care not to judge outsiders,
but it should not hesitate to impose discipline upon its own
members. "For what have I to do with judging outsiders? Is it
not those inside the church whom you are to judge? God judges
those outside. Drive out the wicked person from among you"
(I Cor. 5:12-13; cf. Deut. 17:7). He criticizes the tendency of
Christians to settle their differences before a court of law rather
than within the church:

> When one of you has a grievance against a brother, does he dare
> go to law before the unrighteous instead of the saints? Do you
> not know that the saints will judge the world? And if the world
> is to be judged by you, are you incompetent to try trivial cases?
> Do you not know that we are to judge angels? How much more,
> matters pertaining to this life! (I Cor. 6:1-3)

The New Testament is adamant that church members who
openly flout the moral law of God or who promulgate doctrines
antithetical to the truth of the Gospel are to be censured and
even excommunicated if they show no signs of repentance. The
disciplining of Ananias and Sapphira surely points to this concern for purity in church membership (Ac. 5:1-11). Paul wrote
concerning the man who was practicing incest: "You are to
deliver this man to Satan for the destruction of the flesh, that
his spirit may be saved in the day of the Lord Jesus" (I Cor.
5:5). One possible interpretation of this verse is that the
transgressor by being repudiated by the church might finally be
compelled to repent and thereby recover his salvation. That
excommunication was a common practice in the early church is
also confirmed in this passage from Titus: "As for a man who
is factious, after admonishing him once or twice, have nothing
more to do with him, knowing that such a person is perverted
and sinful; he is self-condemned" (3:10, 11).

The theological and biblical basis for church discipline does
not place in the hand of the church the power to condemn men
to hell. We do not subscribe to the Roman Catholic view that

the church has the power to pronounce anathema. We cannot separate the wheat from the tares, but we are required to judge between the various kinds of wheat. That which has become rotten or that which never ripens must be brought to the attention of the pastor and elders. We cannot pronounce judgment on the eternal salvation of men, but we are called to judge public wickedness. As the apostle declared: "Exhort and reprove with all authority" (Tit. 2:15).

The church has an obligation to exercise discipline, but it must do so in love. We should treat the backslider not as a son of perdition but as a child of God who has strayed from the fold. As Paul said, "Do not look on him as an enemy, but warn him as a brother" (II Thes. 3:15). Christians would do well to adopt Augustine's motto: "Kill the error; love the one erring." The church must always beware of the perils of rigorism and legalism, that is, regarding its own laws as inflexible and as necessary for salvation. It should also be on guard against moralism, i.e., reducing Christian faith to moral maxims or rules. At the same time the church needs to uphold both law and morality. It should remember the statement of our Lord that He came not to abolish the law but to fulfill it (Mt. 5:17). Love supplies us with the motivation for obeying the law, not for abandoning it.

The Reformers, Calvin and Luther, often spoke of the church as being our mother in the faith. A mother must discipline her children precisely because she loves them. Just as parents who have the welfare of their child at heart may not give him supper if he misbehaves, so the church may withhold the Lord's Supper from her errant children. Both Luther and Calvin withheld Communion from those who openly defied church teaching (on such matters as usury and profligacy).

Dietrich Bonhoeffer maintains that the preaching of forgiveness should be accompanied by a call to repentance. And this repentance must be directed to particular sins as well as sin in general.

> Nor is it enough simply to deplore in general terms that the sinfulness of man infects even his good works. It is necessary to point out concrete sins, and to punish and condemn them. This is the proper use of the *power of the keys* ... which the Lord bequeathed to his Church. ... It is essential for the Church to exercise it, for the sake of holiness, for the sake of the sinner and for its own sake. If the Church is to walk worthily of the gospel, part of its duty will be to maintain ecclesiastical discipline. Sanc-

tification means driving out the world from the Church as well as separating the Church from the world.[3]

## CHURCH DISCIPLINE IN HISTORICAL PERSPECTIVE

In the early church, discipline was a matter of course, and frequently the penances imposed upon wrongdoers were quite harsh. Sins that were committed had to be confessed openly before the congregation, and it was this public humiliation that was regarded as the most effective means of discipline. Excommunication was widely practiced, and in some regions the excommunicated were readmitted to church membership through grades of penance.

In medieval Roman Catholicism two kinds of discipline were imposed — one upon the ordinary Christians and the other upon the religious. The latter were regarded as being under the counsels of perfection (celibacy, poverty and obedience) as well as the commandments of God. Among the specific forms of discipline in the Roman church have been the withholding of Communion, excommunication, anathema and the interdict. In the latter the faithful although remaining in communion with the church are barred from certain sacraments and privileges. In Roman Catholic jurisprudence a whole nation can be placed under an interdict, and this has happened on various occasions.

The Protestant Reformers protested against the double standard in morality which permeated the life of the Roman church of that time;[4] in their view all Christians are called to live according to the perfect law of love. Luther as well as Calvin advocated the exercise of church discipline, but in regard to moral conduct the former was not as insistent upon the application of censure and excommunication. Luther's ideal was the free Christian, one who makes his own laws according to the spirit of love. His emphasis was upon self-discipline more than church discipline in the area of morals, although he did not hesitate to admonish wrongdoers in his congregation. On the subject of faith, Luther was much more stringent. He averred that heresy should not be tolerated, and here church discipline was deemed very important. Luther's view that the commandment of love is mandatory only in personal relationships tended

3 Dietrich Bonhoeffer, *The Cost of Discipleship*, trans. R. H. Fuller (London: SCM, 1959), p. 260.

4 The Second Vatican Council has sought to surmount this double standard by declaring that all Christians are called to an apostolic vocation. See *Dogmatic Constitution on the Church*, Chs. IV, V in Walter M. Abbott, ed., *The Documents of Vatican II* (N.Y.: American Press, 1966), pp. 56-72.

to exempt the social and political life of man from the scrutiny of the church. By restricting church discipline to matters of personal faith and private morality Luther, and even more Lutheran theologians subsequent to the Reformation, helped to pave the way for the breakdown of church discipline in modern Protestantism.

Calvin was much more insistent than Luther upon the necessity for church discipline. This was partly due to the influence of Martin Bucer. Calvin's ideal was the disciplined Christian life within a community of discipline. He maintained that all Christians are under the discipline of the moral law, but he allowed for special disciplines such as celibacy so long as they were not held to be meritorious. He believed that the clergy, being examples to their flock, should be under additional disciplines. In his view clergymen should not participate in hunting, gambling, and feasting, nor should they be present at dissolute dancing. He also advocated fasting as a practice suitable for all Christians. According to Calvin fasting serves as a restraint on the flesh, a preparation for prayer and a testimony of one's humiliation. Fasting can be encouraged but not demanded by the church, since such a discipline is basically voluntary. Calvin did not go so far as Bucer in regarding discipline as one of the marks of the true church, together with the Word and sacraments. But he did consider it to be necessary for the full life of the church. He declared that "as the saving doctrine of Christ is the soul of the church, so does discipline serve as its sinews, through which the members of the body hold together, each in its own place."[5]

According to Calvin the consistory (the elders and pastor) are responsible for implementing church discipline. The first step consists in private admonitions. If this is not successful then it should be followed by public renunciation, in the form of censure and excommunication. Those who are notorious violators of God's law are to be barred from the Lord's Supper. A few whose actions and beliefs are a disruptive factor in the whole community should be exiled. Calvin even admitted the possibility of anathema which condemns one to eternal death, but this contravenes the logic of his theology. He generally held that excommunication does not entail a judgment concerning one's eternal salvation; rather it is to be viewed as a practical

[5] John Calvin, *Institutes of the Christian Religion*, ed. John McNeill, trans. Ford Lewis Battles (Philadelphia: Westminster, 1960), IV, 12, 1, p. 1230.

means of disciplining the wayward Christian and it should always offer the possibility of return to the fold on the condition of repentance.

Calvin seeks to avoid all legalism and moralism in his doctrine of church discipline. The disciplined life is not to be seen as meritorious or redemptive. It is the effect and result rather than the source of our salvation. Moreover, according to Calvin, the rules of church discipline are to be applied to all Christians without exception. In his own parish in Geneva he imposed discipline upon the rich and influential as well as the poor. This indeed was the source of much of his trouble in Geneva, and it is one reason why he was compelled to leave the city for a time.

The Heidelberg Catechism reflects the concern for church discipline on the part of the Calvinistic Reformation. In answer to the question concerning the way in which the kingdom of heaven is shut and opened by Christian discipline, the catechism declares:

> Christ commanded that those who bear the Christian name in an unchristian way either in doctrine or in life should be given brotherly admonition. If they do not give up their errors or evil ways, notification is given to the church or to those ordained for this by the church. Then, if they do not change after this warning, they are forbidden to partake of the holy Sacraments and are thus excluded from the communion of the church and by God himself from the kingdom of Christ. However, if they promise and show real amendment, they are received again as members of Christ and of the church.[6]

The left-wing of the Reformation, particularly Anabaptism, was also insistent upon the indispensability of church discipline. The Anabaptists saw the church as a covenantal community which required one to make the promise to live up to the covenantal agreement. Against those who disregarded the covenant and who remained unrepentant, the "ban" was put into effect, which meant expulsion from the congregation of believers. For the most part the ban entailed a loss of privileges within the brotherhood, but sometimes it also involved social ostracism.[7]

Puritanism, which borrowed from Anabaptism but which is

---

6 Allen Miller and M. Eugene Osterhaven, trans., *The Heidelberg Catechism with Commentary*, 400th Anniversary Edition (Philadelphia: United Church Press, 1963), Ques. 85, p. 144. Note that it is not the church that excludes the unrepentant sinner from the kingdom of Christ but God Himself. The most the church can do is to bar him from Holy Communion and the Christian fellowship.

7 See Franklin H. Littell, *The Origins of Sectarian Protestantism* (N.Y.: Macmillan, 1952), pp. 86f.

basically rooted in Calvinism, also envisaged the church as a disciplined community. Modesty and piety were among the virtues held up by the Puritans. Before being admitted to church membership one had to demonstrate that he had indeed experienced a new birth. In New England Puritanism in order to be admitted to the Lord's Supper one had to give evidence of personal piety as well as knowledge of the faith. Richard Baxter gave poignant testimony to the Puritan ideal: "If the holy and unholy are permitted to be sheep of the same fold, without the use of Christian means to difference them, we do defame Christ by it."[8] Excommunication was a common procedure in the Puritan communities. Jonathan Edwards states the rationale for this practice: "The ends of this ecclesiastical censure are: that the church may be kept pure, and the ordinances of God not be defiled; that others may be deterred from wickedness; and that the persons themselves may be reclaimed, and that their souls may be saved."[9]

The principal instrument of church discipline in early Methodism was the class meeting.[10] John Wesley held that to win people without providing them with the care and discipline of a Christian fellowship is to "breed children for the Murderer." The members of the Methodist Societies were divided into classes under a spiritual director. These classes provided the opportunity for Christians to confide in one another and also to receive mutual guidance and admonition. Among the forms of discipline that were practiced in early Methodism were the withholding of the Supper (the lesser ban) and expulsion (the greater ban).

That discipline is generally disregarded in modern Protestantism has already been recognized. Yet provisions for the discipline of unruly and factious members can still be found in the constitutions of many of our larger denominations. For example, in the United Presbyterian Church it is stated that "the session is charged with maintaining the spiritual government of the congregation, for which purpose it has power to inquire into the knowledge and Christian conduct of the mem-

8 Richard Baxter, *The Reformed Pastor,* ed. J. T. Wilkinson (London: Epworth, 1950), 2nd ed. rev., p. 105.

9 Jonathan Edwards, *Devotions of Jonathan Edwards,* ed. Ralph G. Turnbull (Grand Rapids: Baker, 1959), p. 85.

10 See Franklin Littell, "The Methodist Class Meeting as an Instrument of Christian Discipline" in *World Parish* (Feb., 1961), pp. 14-24; and Samuel Emerick, ed., *Spiritual Renewal for Methodism* (Nashville: Methodist Evangelistic Materials, 1958).

bers of the church; to call before it offenders and witnesses; . . .
to decide who shall be members of the church; . . . to admonish,
to rebuke, to suspend or exclude from the sacraments those who
are found to deserve censure; to concert the best measures for
promoting the spiritual interests of the congregation."[11] The
power is there, but it is rarely used.

## AN EXPERIMENT IN CHURCH DISCIPLINE

Church discipline is being restored in some local congregations today, although such churches are very exceptional. In this
section we intend to examine a contemporary experiment in
church discipline in order to ascertain whether the disciplined
community is still a live option in our age.

The Church of the Saviour in Washington, D.C. is one example of a disciplined community in our time.[12] The church was
begun in 1946 by Gordon Cosby and his wife with a membership of nine and a treasury of $30.00. Cosby, an American Bap-
tist minister, had been a chaplain in the airborne division of an
American infantry regiment during World War II. The church
now has less than 90 members, although more than twice this
number are in attendance every Sunday morning. The annual
budget of the church exceeds $65,000; 25% is given to foreign
missions. A large part of this sum is designated for the local
council of churches, the National Council of Churches and the
World Council of Churches. In addition the church sponsors
a guest house for foreign students, a halfway house for alcoholics, a coffee house known as "The Potter's House," and a
house church dedicated to missionary work in suburbia called
the Rockville Congregation. The church has also founded a
renewal center "Dayspring," which includes a retreat house "the
Lodge of the Carpenter," camps for children and adults, and
an amphitheater for religious festivals. This small band of dedicated Christians is also planning to establish a spiritual sanitarium for the mentally and emotionally disturbed. The church,
which draws its members from various races and social classes,
has no official denominational ties.

How can a group this small be such a spiritual powerhouse?

11 From *The Constitution of the United Presbyterian Church in the United
States of America* 1964-65 (Philadelphia: The Office of the General Assembly of the United Presbyterian Church, 1963), "Form of Government," Chapter XI, No. 6, pp. 125-126.

12 For the story of this experiment see Elizabeth O'Connor, *Call to Commitment* (N.Y.: Harper & Row, 1963) and also by the same author, *Journey
Inward, Journey Outward* (N.Y.: Harper & Row, 1968).

The answer partly lies in the strict membership requirements and also in the disciplined life of the congregation. Before one can become a member of the Church of the Saviour, he must undergo one-and-a-half years of training and instruction. He is expected to enroll in the school of Christian living sponsored by the church and graduate with satisfactory marks. Biblical studies comprise the core of the curriculum. Moreover, every year he must formally recommit himself to the service of Christ as a working-member of the church.

Once having become a member one is obligated to join one of the mission or fellowship groups in the church. Unlike most churches the Church of the Saviour has no social organizations as such. Every fellowship group is devoted to a special mission project and is generally open to any member, whether that person be single or married, male or female, colored or white, young or old. For a fellowship group to exist there must be no less than four and no more than twelve members. The group must be approved by the Council of the Church before it can function as a part of the church's mission. The retreat center, the coffee house, the restoration corps, whose members repair slum tenements, the guest house for foreign students, and a program dedicated to finding foster homes for children of indigent parents are among the mission projects which are open to the members. The Church of the Saviour has recently instituted a service of ordination to the lay ministry thereby giving substance to the Reformation doctrine of the priesthood of believers.

The new member is called upon to live a life in keeping with his holy vocation. He must formally pledge himself to abide by certain disciplines including daily prayer, tithing, daily study of the Scripture, weekly worship and the daily expression of Christian love in redeeming service. He is encouraged also to place himself under a Spiritual Director, a person of spiritual sensitivity and wisdom. The members of this church see themselves as soldiers of Christ in a world where evil powers still run rampant. They view the church as a school of discipline and training which equips them for the service of God in the world. In answer to the question "How is your church growing?" they could very well point to the words of Scripture, "In the grace and knowledge of our Lord and Saviour Jesus Christ" (II Pet. 3:18).

The fact that the Church of the Saviour is not affiliated with any denomination may give us a clue to its success as a disciplined and vigorous congregation. A church that is not itself under the discipline of a bishop or presbyter or synod might be more free to experiment in new forms of ministry and service. Perhaps one answer to the dearth of vitality in the church today lies in giving the local church more freedom and opportunity to pioneer in various areas. Our need is for both greater discipline in doctrine and morals and greater liberty concerning the ways by which we can witness to the Gospel and implement discipline.

This is not to imply that the Church of the Saviour is beyond criticism. Some of its recent literature can lead one to question whether it is solidly anchored in a theology of the Word of God that stands over against cultural values and ideals.[13] At the same time an experiment such as this should certainly be emulated, since it shows the possibilities that are open to a local church in the area of Christian mission.

## NEED FOR THE RESTORATION OF CHURCH DISCIPLINE

One of the needs in the area of church discipline today is the tightening of ordination examinations. Too many young men are being ordained into the ministry who are not evangelical in their religious convictions and indeed who have no creed whatsoever. In some churches the examinations deal mainly with polity and church history. But certainly it is not knowledge of the church as an institution that should be the primary concern. It is personal piety and fidelity to the Scriptural message that should command our attention, but how many presbyteries, associations and congregations even inquire about such matters? In this same connection congregations should not extend a call to a minister until they are sure of his doctrinal beliefs. But what most congregations are interested in today is whether the minister is married, young, good at working with youth and a respectable citizen. Yet these are cultural values, surely not the biblical standards for the Christian ministry.

We also need higher standards for church membership. We should no longer speak of inactive members or of inactive faith. Such terms are blatantly un-Scriptural. Those who no longer regularly attend the services of worship and who do not contribute substantially to the work and mission of the church should be

---

13 For example we find it difficult to accept Elizabeth O'Connor's contention in her book *Journey Inward, Journey Outward* that self-discovery is the precondition to God-discovery. In the biblical understanding one must first be awakened to the love of God revealed in Jesus Christ before he can know himself.

removed from membership rolls. Moreover, no person should be accepted for membership until he has been made thoroughly aware of the responsibilities it involves. The person seeking membership should also be given instruction in biblical history and church doctrine. He should be informed that church membership entails not only right belief but a Christian life. Indeed, every member should be a full participant in the mission of the church. Don Benedict has rightly declared: "The basis of church membership must be more than acceptance of Christ as Lord and Savior. The basis of any call to membership must include a commitment to Servanthood in God's world."[14]

The church today also needs to examine critically its policy of indiscriminate baptism and communion. Only those children should be baptized whose parents and sponsors are themselves actively engaged in the work of the church. A minimum standard would be that at least one parent be a full member of the church and that only this parent be permitted to take public vows on behalf of the child. Anyone leading a life of flagrant disobedience to God's law and who is unwilling to change should be barred from the Lord's Supper. To be sure, we are all sinners, but only some are unrepentant sinners. We need to take seriously these words of Bonhoeffer: "If we come to hear the Word of God and receive the sacrament without first being reconciled with our neighbors, we shall come to our own damnation."[15]

This brings us again to the subject of excommunication. We have already pointed to the solid biblical foundations for this practice. Our view is that it sorely needs to be reinstated. Yet one must proceed with caution in this area mainly because of the dangers of legalism and "playing god." A prime motivation for excommunication should be none other than Christian love, particularly for the transgressor. Our goal should be to win him back into the fold of the church by means of disciplinary action. Other legitimate aims of excommunication are that God may be honored and that the purity and welfare of the church be maintained.

It may be wise to distinguish between various kinds of censure as does a recent statement on worship and discipline drawn up by Southern Presbyterian and Reformed churchmen.[16] The

14 Stephen Rose, ed., *Who's Killing the Church?* (N.Y.: Association, 1966), p. 46.

15 Dietrich Bonhoeffer, *The Cost of Discipleship*, p. 118.

16 See John A. Fulton, Norman E. Thomas, et al., *Proposals Regarding the Worship and Work of the Church and Its Discipline*, 1967.

first stage of discipline can be considered admonition which
is a formal reproof of an offender by a church court, warning
him of his guilt and advising him to be more watchful in the
future. A second stage can be described as suspension in which
the offender is temporarily excluded from the sacraments. Excommunication should probably be reserved for only the most
opprobrious crimes, and it should entail a complete severance
from the fellowship of the church. There should also be a place
for deposition, which means the removal of an officer in the
church from his office.

What are some things that might merit censure and discipline
in our time? Surely immoral conduct could be mentioned, since
this was one of the primary causes of expulsion in the New
Testament. But we should have in mind not only immoral conduct in personal matters but also in public matters. Those who
earn their living by working in a nuclear or germ war plant,
for example, probably merit admonition from the church. Busi-
nessmen who exploit their employees by keeping their stores
open on Sunday should surely be censured for their conduct.
Politicians who appeal to racial and religious prejudice should
also be threatened with suspension or excommunication. At
the same time the sins of the flesh, e.g., sexual promiscuity and
perversion, drunkenness and drug addiction should by no means
be overlooked. It is a tragic indictment of the modern church
that it simply winks at wrongdoing in areas of sexual morality
and seems unwilling to apply even the minimal disciplinary action against transgressors.

Still another area where discipline could be applied is that
of heresy. To be sure, the church must be equally wary of heresy
hunters, and it should always respect freedom and independent
thinking. An index of censored books is out of place in an evangelical church, since all points of view need to be considered
by the clergy and also the educated laity. Yet no minister
who openly repudiates the cardinal tenets of the faith should
be permitted to express his views from the pulpit. Nor should
informed laymen who hold positions of influence within the
church be allowed to disseminate views which are clearly contrary to the Scriptural mandate. One must distinguish between the possibility of being mistaken in one's theology
(which we all are to some degree) and being fanatically dedicated to error. As the new Presbyterian and Reformed proposal
on discipline rightly states: "Heresy and schism may be of such
a nature as to warrant Deposition; but errors should be care-

fully considered whether they strike at the vitals of religion, and are industriously spread, or whether they arise from the weakness of human understanding, and are not likely to do much injury."[17] All Christians have at least one foot in some kind of heresy, but when this heresy becomes a new Gospel (as e.g., "the Gospel of Christian atheism"), when it becomes a threat to the confessional integrity of the church, then the church must take action. Bonhoeffer has some wise remarks on this matter:

> It is not always easy to see where a legitimate school of thought ends and heresy begins. That is why a doctrine may be tolerated in one Church and proscribed as heresy in another. . . . But once a heresy has become an open scandal it must of necessity be proscribed. The heretical teacher must be excommunicated and all personal intercourse with him avoided.[18]

What is stressed in most of our churches is not church discipline but self-discipline. Yet self-discipline cannot be maintained apart from the discipline of a larger community. We need to be reminded of the Scriptural truth that we are responsible not only for ourselves but also for our brother. We are in one sense our brother's keeper, and this means that when the occasion presents itself we must be willing to admonish and reprove him in love. But we must also be humble, since but for God's grace we also might have fallen into the sin that afflicts our brother. Paul's words are very apropos: "Brethren, if a man is overtaken in any trespass, you who are spiritual should restore him in a spirit of gentleness. Look to yourself, lest you too be tempted" (Gal. 6:1).

It is imperative that we recover the idea of the church as a covenantal community. We as the people of the church need to covenant with God and also with one another in order to fulfill our holy vocation. New covenants are necessitated by the new era in which we find ourselves, and this may mean promises to forswear racial discrimination, nuclear war and the new morality.

Every church should seek a balance between peace, unity and purity. This can be converted into an argument against church discipline, since discipline disturbs the peace and unity of the church. Yet we must bear in mind that true peace and unity lie in a common faith in Jesus Christ and an outgoing love to our neighbor. In order to attain that higher peace and true unity we must at the same time insist upon purity and fidelity. We must not do ... out of contempt for our neighbor but precisely

17 *Ibid.*, p. 63.
18 Dietrich Bonhoeffer, *The Cost of Discipleship*, p. 228.

out of love for him and a concern for his eternal salvation. May we seek to restore a discipline in our churches that is biblically anchored and relevant to the needs and problems of our day.

# SEVEN:

# A NEW KIND
# OF CONFIRMATION

## THE STATUS OF CONFIRMATION TODAY

The rite of confirmation is now under reappraisal throughout Christendom. This is true particularly among Lutherans and Reformed, who have sought to strengthen this rite and at the same time anchor it more solidly in the biblical revelation. But the churches that stand in the tradition of evangelical revivalism are also asking whether confirmation can have a place in their ecclesiastical life, since there seems to be need for a special consecration to Christ particularly on the part of children who have grown up in the family of the church.

In the Lutheran and old Reformed churches today confirmation is generally a graduation exercise. It is intended to signify a graduation into Christian maturity, but too often it amounts to a celebration of the arrival of the child to social maturity. In many cases it entails a graduation out of the family of the church, since the child now views himself as accepted by church and society and as being under no further obligations to his Lord and Savior. This, of course, is a travesty of the rite of confirmation, but this attitude is very widespread.

In the churches that stand in the free church and revival traditions, confirmation (when the term is used) is usually nothing more than membership instruction. This applies even to Presbyterian churches which have generally divorced the rite from any sacramental connotations. In the churches of these traditions, which embrace most of American Protestantism, confirmation is related neither to divine election nor to the strengthening work of the Holy Spirit. The fatal flaw in this approach is that church membership is seen to involve nothing more than a subjective decision. The church is envisaged as a gathered community, gathered out of the world, rather than a sacramental community in which one is baptized into a fellowship of service. There is truth in both these conceptions of the church, but withdrawal from the world must always be held in balance with active involvement in the world.

In Roman Catholicism confirmation is understood as a sacrament which signifies the fulfillment or perfection of baptism. It is regarded as "the sacrament of the messianic fullness of the Spirit."[1] One catechism states: "Confirmation brings the Holy Spirit to our souls, increases the grace of God within us, and imprints on us a spiritual mark which can never be effaced."[2] According to the Roman Catechism (1566) confirmation also pardons and remits sin.

At the same time in the Roman Catholic church children are generally admitted to full membership apart from confirmation. As soon as they reach the age of discernment they can receive Holy Communion, even though they have not been confirmed. The practice in Spain is an exception, since there people are confirmed as infants. Although baptism is regarded very highly and is considered sufficient for Holy Communion, there seems to be a deemphasis of baptism in the Catholic church, since the fullness of the Spirit is not believed to come until confirmation. The fact that every priest can baptize but only bishops can confirm also seems to detract from the significance of baptism.[3] The fact that countless numbers are lost to the church after confirmation is a sign that drastic reforms are necessary in this area of church life.

The Anglican church is presently divided concerning the meaning of confirmation. The Anglo-Catholics generally hold that in confirmation we receive the gift of the Spirit, and some even refer to confirmation as the sacrament of the sealing of the Spirit. One catechism states that in confirmation one receives the gift of the Spirit "to complete what he began in Baptism, and to give strength for the Christian life" (Anglican *Revised Catechism*). Evangelical Anglicans contend that the gift of the Spirit is fully given in baptism and faith, and confirmation is a rite of personal dedication to Christ. As in the Roman church only the bishops administer confirmation.

In the Eastern Orthodox churches confirmation is viewed as an integral part of the rite of initiation, being administered with baptism. It is generally seen as the rite of the sealing of the Spirit. One is baptized by immersion with water and sealed by the anointing with oil or chrism. The general practice in the

---

1 Burkhard Neunheuser, *Baptism and Confirmation*, trans. John J. Hughes (N.Y.: Herder & Herder, 1964), p. 251.

2 Joseph Malloy, *A Catechism For Inquirers* (Glen Rock, N.J.: Paulist Press, 1965), p. 36.

3 Priests can confirm in an emergency situation where no bishop is present.

Orthodox churches is the baptism and confirmation of infants. An evangelical criticism of the Orthodox position is that confirmation is not related in any way to personal consecration and dedication in the world. Nor is it related to catechetical instruction. Confirmation like baptism in their churches becomes automatic and mechanical and is almost totally devoid of ethical significance.

## CONFIRMATION IN THE HISTORY OF THE CHURCH

In the New Testament church the general practice was believers' baptism by immersion often accompanied by the laying on of hands. The baptism itself was believed to bestow the gift of the Spirit, and the additional rite of laying on of hands was regarded as communicating certain charismata of the Spirit which equipped the Christian for his mission in the world.[4] In baptism believers are buried with Christ and sealed with the Spirit unto the day of redemption. There was no special rite of confirmation subsequent to baptism which was thought to complete that sacrament.

By the third century the baptismal rite of initiation became separated into various parts. This was due mainly to the rise of infant baptism and the growth of the church which prevented bishops from being present at every baptism. The baptism with water was equated with the new birth, regeneration, the washing away of sin, and it was followed often immediately but sometimes much later by the imposition of hands and the anointing with oil that was believed to confer the fullness of the Spirit. Among most of the fathers the sealing of the Spirit still referred basically to baptism, but later the sealing was thought to take place at confirmation or the laying on of hands. The term *confirmatio* was used for the first time officially at the Council of Orange (441). Confirmation was not officially defined as a separate sacrament until the Council of Florence (1439). The views of Thomas Aquinas were determinative for later Catholic theology in this area. Thomas did not refer to confirmation as a sealing of the Spirit, but he contended that it conveyed the sevenfold gift of the Spirit. He also regarded it as the outward badge or sign of the Christian soldier.

In later medieval Catholic theology confirmation was believed to be a means of empowering grace which perfects or completes baptism. It was said that one becomes a child of God at baptism

---

[4] See G. W. H. Lampe, *The Seal of the Spirit* (London: Longmans, Green, 1956), 2nd ed., pp. 46f., 306f.

and a soldier of Christ at confirmation. Confirmation moreover places on the believer an indelible mark, the seal of the Holy Spirit. It also effects the remission of sins. The Holy Spirit is already present at baptism, but He does not complete or perfect His work until confirmation.

The Protestant Reformers, Luther and Calvin, strongly reacted against the Catholic sacrament of confirmation. In their view confirmation is not a sacrament because it was not instituted by Christ. Moreover, they contended that the Spirit is given in baptism and faith; there is no second outpouring of the Spirit in a rite subsequent to baptism. At the same time they sought to lay the foundation for an evangelical confirmation. In the theology of the Reformers confirmation is associated with catechetical instruction. Luther even called it a *ceremonia sacramentalis* (a sacramental ceremony). John Knox wished to retain the rite of confirmation and also the benediction (blessing) by the laying on of hands.

The real fathers of Evangelical Confirmation are Erasmus, Martin Bucer, Martin Chemnitz, and Philip Spener. Bucer was the first to develop a new liturgical rite of confirmation. All these theologians emphasized the necessity for a public reaffirmation of the baptismal vows, but it was the Pietists in particular who recognized the indispensability for personal consecration and rededication. Confirmation in Evangelical churches has even been called the child of Pietism, but this is perhaps an overstatement. The theological foundations for confirmation were laid before the advent of Pietism, but it was not until Pietism that confirmation became an accepted rite in the life of Protestantism. What is most important in Pietist theology is the vow of the child to live a pious life. Confirmation was seen as being supplementary and complementary to baptism. Schleiermacher, who partly stands in the tradition of Pietism, regarded baptism as incomplete apart from the response of faith and confirmation. The views of John Nevin and Philip Schaff of the Mercersburg movement in America were very similar.

The modern rite of confirmation is rooted not only in Pietism but also in the Enlightenment. The Age of Rationalism (18th century) exerted an important influence upon the development of confirmation within Protestantism. Confirmation was seen as an occasion for a decision to lead a completely responsible and ethical life. It was understood as a declaration of maturity. For all practical purposes it became a rite of puberty, a Protestant Bar Mitzwah. It celebrated the arrival of the child to the age of responsibility. This understanding of confirmation is still very much in vogue in cultural Protestantism.

## CONFIRMATION AS THE ORDINATION OF THE LAITY

In line with the theology of the Reformation we hold that confirmation should not be viewed as a supplementation or fulfillment of baptism. The gift of the Spirit is conferred in baptism and faith (Ac. 2:38). Baptism indeed is the sign both of divine election and man's conversion. Baptism in order to be complete must entail repentance and faith on the part of the one baptized, but such repentance is not symbolized by a post-baptismal rite but rather by baptism itself.

Dom Gregory Dix, the noted Anglican Benedictine scholar, draws a distinction between baptism into the body of Christ and the Pentecostal baptism of the Spirit.[5] He maintains that in the New Testament the bath of immersion signifies the washing away of sin, and the imposition of hands (which he associates with confirmation) confers the sealing of the Spirit. This view is also subscribed to by Lionel Thornton, another Anglican Benedictine. Their position is hotly contested by the Anglican theologian G. W. Lampe who maintains that the imposition of hands in the New Testament does not confer the Spirit anew but only special gifts of the Spirit.[6] Our sympathies lie with Dr. Lampe.

What then is confirmation? We affirm that it is not a sacrament instituted by Christ as a means of salvation. It does not signify a baptism with fire which complements water baptism as Bernard Haering and some other Catholic theologians imply. But it can be regarded as a sacramental means of grace which strengthens one for service in the kingdom. It equips one for an apostolic vocation in the world. We could subscribe to Father Bernard Cooke's description of confirmation as an intensification of the baptismal character rather than the conferring of a second sacramental character.[7]

What is the New Testament basis for confirmation? One might point to Ac. 13:3 where Paul, after having already been baptized and ordained, receives the laying on of hands anew for a special commission. In II Cor. 1:21 Paul declares: "But it is

---

[5] See Dom Gregory Dix, *The Theology of Confirmation in Relation to Baptism* (Westminster: Dacra Press, 1946).

[6] G. W. Lampe, *op. cit.*

[7] Bernard J. Cooke, *Christian Sacraments and Christian Personality* (N.Y.: Holt, Rinehart & Winston, 1965), p. 95.

God who established us with you in Christ and has commissioned us." This may possibly refer to baptism but more than likely it signifies a special anointing of the Spirit for a particular service. Again the apostle writes that he hopes to impart to his hearers "some spiritual gift" to strengthen them in their vocation (Rom. 1:11). In the New Testament church it seems that the laying on of hands was associated with various rites including baptism, ordination and a special commissioning for Christian service. There are also passages which urge Christians to consecrate themselves anew (Rom. 12:1; Eph. 4:22-24) and confirm their divine calling (II Pt. 1:10). Such passages do not refer to a special rite, but nevertheless they are relevant to this discussion, since they provide the theological rationale for a strengthening and confirming rite by which believers are empowered for service in the kingdom.

Confirmation should be understood not as a rite which admits one to church membership but rather as an act by which we assume responsibility for our church membership. It is baptism and faith which make one a member of the body of Christ, but we then need to reaffirm our baptismal commitment. Confirmation can be seen as a rite by which one is admitted to the full responsibilities and privileges of church membership. It is the rite that equips us for service in the kingdom of God.

The question is currently being debated as to whether confirmation grants one the privilege of partaking of Holy Communion. It first should be said that the principal purpose of confirmation is not to prepare one for Communion but rather for a mature commitment to kingdom service. Yet confirmation should be associated with Communion, since consecration to Christ and Communion are integrally related. It can be said that the three components of classical Evangelical confirmation are examination (catechization), the laying on of hands and consecration, and Holy Communion. Luther and Calvin both made profession of faith the precondition for Holy Communion. Their emphasis was upon a personal act of confession by which one was admitted to Communion. One suggestion today is that confirmation should be divided into two stages, and the first stage should be viewed as a preparation for Communion.[8] In this period we are given catechetical instruction, particularly on the meaning of the sacraments. Such instruction could even be regarded as pre-confirmation, since we are not

8 *Confirmation: A Study Document,* trans. Walter G. Tillmanns (Minneapolis: Augsburg, 1963), p. 83.

confirmed until sometime later. The second stage should be characterized by a study concerning the implications of Christian faith for life in the world today. What should be given the young person is a course in Christian vocation. This second stage might be climaxed in a rite of Confirmation with confession of faith, intercession and consecration.

Our recommendation is that the catechetical and doctrinal instruction in the faith be solid and that it should extend at least over a two-year period. There is a place for memorizing in a confirmation class, despite what some Christian educators assert. Above all the child should not be encouraged to write his own confession of faith, since this is not the purpose of these classes. What is important is that the child or young person understand the faith into which he was baptized, the faith of the church through the ages. It is this faith to which he is required to give assent, not only with his mind but with his whole being. He should be encouraged to raise questions in the confirmation class but for the purpose of clarifying the doctrine of Scripture. Christianity is not a general quest for truth but rather a definitive witness to the truth which is clearly revealed in Scripture and acknowledged by the catechisms and confessions of the Reformation. What is needed in a confirmation class is the voice of authority as well as a teaching method that will elicit interest and even enthusiasm.

Confirmation can best be understood today as an ordination of the laity for service in the world.[9] It signifies a second movement of the Spirit by which we are turned in the direction of engagement in Christian mission. The ordination to the ministry of the Word and sacraments can be understood as a third movement of the Spirit. Confirmation is not the occasion by which we receive a deeper dose of the Spirit but rather by which we are pointed by the Spirit in a new direction.

Johann Christoph Blumhardt spoke of two conversions, one to the church and the second to the world. But these must not be seen as equivalent to baptism and confirmation. The act of baptism and faith already entails a dedication to the service of our neighbor. Moreover, at confirmation we make a decision to enter upon missionary service in the ranks of the church for the sake of the world. The churches can learn from the Salvation

---

9 I acknowledge my indebtedness to Max Thurian's *Consecration of the Layman*, trans. W. J. Kerrigan (Baltimore: Helicon, 1963). Unlike Thurian, however, I see water baptism as being the sign and seal of the baptism of the Spirit.

Army, which has a special rite of Commissioning that follows conversion to Christ. We are already soldiers of Christ, but now we are sent forth into the field of battle. Our conversion to Christ can be said to be deepened and renewed at confirmation.

Just as there is a definite relationship between Confirmation and Holy Communion, so there is an even deeper relationship between Confirmation and Holy Baptism. Confirmation makes little sense apart from infant baptism. It presupposes both baptism and faith. Indeed, before a child is confirmed, he should be examined in order to ascertain whether he now possesses faith. Confirmation is the renewal of the baptismal covenant; it is a remembrance of our baptism. It should not be viewed as the fulfillment or culmination of baptism; rather it is a dedication to the faith into which we were baptized. It is not necessary for salvation, but it is a passport for victorious living.

When we speak of confirmation we generally have in mind the children of believers, who have been baptized and who have been nurtured in the covenant community. For adults who have never been baptized and who now seek membership in the church, the only rite that is necessary is baptism preceded by catechetical instruction. These persons can be said to receive the Spirit in the twofold act of decision and baptism. Indeed, baptism is also the act by which they are empowered by the Spirit for their life-vocation. There may be a place for an adult confirmation rite in the case of those who have been baptized as infants but who have fallen away from the faith and who now desire church membership. Such persons should only be accepted into the church on the basis of a public profession of faith after a period of instruction in the Christian fundamentals.

Confirmation has traditionally been associated with Pentecost which signifies the outpouring of the Holy Spirit upon the church. We have already maintained that baptism is the authentic sacrament of Pentecost, but confirmation also may be related to Pentecost in that in this rite we petition the Spirit for illumination and power to lead a life of service and witness. Confirmation might also be associated with Epiphany, since it signalizes mission to the world. In order to underscore confirmation as the rite of Christian apostolate (Cooke), churches might do well to confirm their young people on Epiphany Sunday.

Evangelical confirmation should be viewed not as a graduation into adulthood, even Christian adulthood, but as a commissioning to missionary service. It is not the climax of the Christian pilgrimage but rather a setting forth on Christian mission. It can be viewed as a graduation into a missionary fellowship oriented about definite tasks and needs in the world. It involves a decision that gives specific direction to our life-vocation. For this reason some scholars maintain that it is better to postpone confirmation until the later teens. But an argument against this is that children today are soon caught up into the youth culture and need to be anchored in a public confession of faith if they are to survive as Christian men and women. It should be recognized that our vocation is to be servants of Christ; it does not refer to any specific occupation or line of work. We can be decided concerning our vocation and yet remain undecided concerning the way in which we seek to live out this vocation. To be sure, confirmation as we have reinterpreted it concerns the direction of our vocation as well as the vocation itself, but the precise manner in which this is realized need not be determined at the time of confirmation.

What is needed in the church today is for our confirmation as well as our baptism to be renewed. Some churches make a place for a public act of renewal at their New Year's service. The New Year indeed is the time for resolutions, and the church might capitalize on this fact. We might also institute special ceremonies of commissioning which might signalize new departures in Christian service.

The Christian life is one of pilgrimage. Confirmation is neither the beginning nor the end of this pilgrimage. But it is an act of consecration which determines or shapes the direction of this pilgrimage throughout the rest of our life. The Lutheran churches in Eastern Germany have recognized the importance of confirmation in giving direction and guidance to their young people. The Bible verse which is inscribed on the Confirmation certificate of each child has proved a veritable blessing in many cases.[10] The Communist Party has also seen the significance of this rite and consequently has tried to inaugurate secular confirmations in competition to Evangelical Confirmation. What we should seek is not the abandonment of this rite but its reappraisal and deepening in the light of Scripture and the contemporary experience of the church.

---

[10] For the significance of the rite of Confirmation in Eastern Germany today see the motion picture *Question 7* produced by the Louis De Rochemont Associates.

EIGHT:

# NEW FORMS OF THE CHURCH

## CRITICISMS OF THE INSTITUTIONAL CHURCH

In the past decade the institutional church has been subjected to scathing criticism. Some of its critics complain that the church has become too worldly whereas others contend that the church is too isolated from the world. As we shall see, these criticisms are not necessarily antithetical.

According to Gibson Winter the parish church has lost contact with the dire needs and problems of the inner city; moreover, it is in the inner city where the action is.[1] Winter's argument is that the parish church has become family-centered rather than world-centered. Its overriding concern has been to cultivate piety rather than to give itself for the world in servanthood. It has focused its attention upon the local school, the nurture of children and emotional stability rather than the needs and suffering of the despised and forsaken. Winter speaks of the "suburban captivity of the church" by which he means the capitulation of the church to the biases and trivialities of suburban middle class culture.

Other theologians also are pointing to the ideological nature of institutional Christendom. H. Richard Niebuhr contends that the sources of our denominations are not doctrinal so much as cultural.[2] In his view the American church is presently in bondage to capitalism.[3] Cardinal Saliège has made a similar indictment of the Catholic church in France, maintaining that the churches in his country are almost wholly divorced from the working class.

A growing number of voices are also being raised in protest against the developing bureaucracy in the mainline denominations. John Fry complains that most of the benevolence giving

---

[1] See Gibson Winter, *The Suburban Captivity of the Churches* (Garden City, N.Y.: Doubleday, 1961) and his *The New Creation As Metropolis* (N.Y.: Macmillan, 1963).

[2] See his *The Social Sources of Denominationalism* (N.Y.: Holt, 1929).

[3] See H. Richard Niebuhr, Wilhelm Pauck and Francis Miller, *The Church Against the World* (N.Y.: Willett, Clark, 1935).

in the United Presbyterian church is being channeled towards the maintaining of the denominational superstructure.[4] Harvey Cox avers that the churches today seem bent not on service to the world but on the accumulation of property and power. Colin Williams deplores what he calls "heretical structures." In his view the institutional church assumes this character when it diverts from the real task of Christian mission. The church must allow "the *forms* of her renewed life to grow around the *shapes of world need.*"[5] Our problem is that "the local residence congregation is so turned inward that it is often well-nigh impossible to reverse its direction in order that its life may flow outward into the structure of the world's need."[6]

John Robinson, the former Bishop of Woolwich, also sees outmoded structures as constituting the real threat to the life of the church today. He inveighs against what he terms "structural fundamentalism."

> The real trouble is not in the fact that the Church is too rich but that it has become heavily institutionalized, with a crushing investment in maintenance. It has the characteristics of the dinosaur and the battleship. It is saddled with a plant and a programme beyond its means, so that it is absorbed in problems of supply and preoccupied with survival.[7]

## CHANGES IN THE LOCAL CHURCH

In contradistinction to some of the radical theologians, we hold that the parish church is here to stay. At the same time one should recognize that it is gravely limited in its outreach. There is a need today for new kinds of structures within the local church as well as apart from the church.

It cannot be denied that the great majority of the organizations in the church today are much more cultural than spiritual. What we have are clubs based on common interests rather than fellowships of concern bound by a common faith. Many of our church organizations are segregated on the basis of class, sex and race thereby contradicting the Pauline dictum that in Christ there is neither Jew nor Greek, slave nor free, male nor female (Gal. 3:28). A good example of a club functioning under church auspices is the Mariners (in the Presbyterian church), which is

---

[4] John Fry, "The Denominational Dollar" in *Who's Killing the Church?*, ed. Stephen C. Rose (N.Y.: Association, 1966), pp. 59-67.

[5] Colin Williams, *Where In The World?* (N.Y.: National Council of Churches, 1963), p. 59.

[6] *Ibid.,* p. 12.

[7] John Robinson, *The New Reformation?* (Philadelphia: Westminster, 1965), p. 26.

limited on the basis of age and marital status. Any group that is specifically directed to young married couples will almost invariably be ideological and discriminatory because of the immense importance that is attached to status and background.

The way in which the local church supports itself is also something to be deplored. Instead of inculcating in their members the precepts of Christian stewardship, too many churches seek to promote their program by bazaars, bingo and dinners. There is a place for fellowship suppers in the church but not banquets for the purpose of raising money. Another danger in holding banquets in the church is that of overeating, and gluttony should still be seen as one of the seven deadly sins. We would do well to heed St. Paul's admonition: "For the kingdom of God does not mean food and drink but righteousness and peace and joy in the Holy Spirit" (Rom. 14:17).

In our view only five types of organization have a place in the parish church. Each of these should be concerned with one of these themes: Christian apostolate or evangelism, Christian nurture, Good Samaritan service, prayer and social action. Moreover, such groups should be open to all members, young and old, single and married, rich and poor. The tie that will bind the group together is not common cultural interests but rather a burning passion to serve Jesus Christ. No member should be compelled to join any one of these fellowships, but he should definitely be encouraged. Catechetical instruction and Sunday School training properly belong under the category of Christian nurture. Church choirs might be considered an arm of the Christian apostolate. The social action group should take care not to enter into partisan politics, but it should not be afraid to give guidance to the members of the church on issues that are palpably moral and spiritual.

Wesley Baker in his *The Split-Level Fellowship* calls for a new structure for the parish.[8] His view is that pastors should expend their energies in educating the core of the truly committed. He envisions church membership in various levels into which one graduates on the basis of his knowledge of the faith and his willingness to make additional sacrifices. Baker is thinking in the right direction when he sees that the minister cannot do everything and be everything and that consequently there must be a trained corps of dedicated Christians to accomplish the tasks that were formerly allotted to the clergy. But he places

---

8 See Wesley Baker, *The Split-Level Fellowship* (Philadelphia: Westminster, 1965).

too much emphasis upon instruction in the faith and not enough on piety and the Holy Spirit. Also he cheapens baptism by maintaining that only an interest in Christianity is necessary for the first level of church membership.

The historic churches can learn from the Seventh Day Adventists on how to put a local congregation to good use. Each Adventist congregation organizes a "Dorcas" society whose members engage in activities similar to those undertaken by the St. Vincent de Paul Society and the Salvation Army. The Dorcas members meet frequently to make bandages, repair clothing and collect food. Within every community the Adventists often sponsor free first aid classes. A sizable proportion of the members of each local congregation are employed full time by the church either as missionaries, teachers, printers, nurses or doctors. This is made possible by the practice of tithing which is scrupulously followed. In addition the members of the church meet regularly for Bible study and missionary strategy.

## PARA-PAROCHIAL FORMS

In addition to new structures in the local parish there is a need for para-parochial, extra-ecclesiastical or extra-congregational forms and structures. The new wine of the Gospel needs always to be put in new wineskins, and this means that the hope of the church lies in something other than the denominational organization. Troeltsch has stated: "It is germ-cells of a new spiritual freshness, power, concentration, and discipline, which have everywhere to be formed against the crudity, shallowness, and vulgarity of a trivialized or caricatured, increasingly disintegrated and desolate civilization."[9] Another sociologist of religion, Peter Berger, suggests that spiritual renewal if it comes will take place outside the institutional structure of the church, although not wholly apart from it.[10] The new para-parochial forms should have as their purpose not simply to meet worldly need but rather to serve the Gospel proclamation. Moreover, the worldly need that they seek to meet should be primarily the spiritual need for the salvation of Jesus Christ. What are called for are not simply new forms but evangelical forms, for it is only the evangelical message of the cross that can revitalize the church and prepare the way for a new world.

---

[9] Ernst Troeltsch, *Christian Thought: Its History and Application*, ed. Baron Von Hügel (N.Y.: Meridian Books, 1957), p. 143.

[10] Peter Berger, *The Noise of Solemn Assemblies* (Garden City, N.Y.: Doubleday, 1961), pp. 170, 173, 177.

It was the movement of Evangelical Pietism that sought to create new forms of service and witness in the churches of the Reformation, forms that would still be in continuity with the church. The Pietist strategy was the conventicle which constituted a church within the church *(ecclesiola in ecclesia)*, a gathering of people who met during the week or on Sunday evenings for the purposes of Bible study and devotion. Sometimes the conventicle took the form of a mission service in which people were challenged to conversion and rededication. The class meeting of Methodism was similar except that it formed an integral part of the local church itself. It signified a cell group that came together for purposes of mutual edification and discipline. The Methodist class meeting within the Anglican church was more or less a para-parochial form, but in Methodism it became a part of the life of the local church.

Retreat houses or spiritual sanitariums have arisen both out of Pietism and Catholic movements within Protestantism. We are speaking here particularly of Evangelical retreat houses, although we should bear in mind that this form of spiritual renewal has had a long history in Catholicism. There is a special need today for retreat houses within Protestantism, since our people are too much of the world to be effective witnesses in the world. We should seek to build centers for spiritual rehabilitation, study and meditation. Too many Protestant "retreats" are not really retreats but conferences, and most of our people return from such meetings worn out rather than spiritually renewed. It is imperative that Protestants learn again the discipline of silence which is sadly lacking in most of our retreat conferences. The Christian today needs periodic withdrawal from the many influences beating upon him in the culture so that he can gain the spiritual strength and freedom to become actively involved in the world. It is necessary to withdraw from the smog-blanketed city of the world to the hills in order to rethink our mission and receive power from on high; then we can return to the city and be smog-fighters. The Ecumenical House of Prayer in Benifold, England, a retreat house supervised by a pastor, his wife, and a few aides, has proved to be a source of spiritual vitality and renewal.

Houses of mercy are also greatly needed in our time, including hospitals, orphanages, epileptic homes, homes for the mentally retarded, and sanitariums for the emotionally distraught. Such houses of mercy are very common in the traditions of Catholicism and Protestant Pietism, but it is interesting to note that in areas dominated by Buddhism, Hinduism and other non-Christian religions, they are practically nonexistent. Such centers exemplify the Scriptural truth that salvation entails the healing of the whole man, and not merely his soul. Both church and community hospitals in our nation are in a period of crisis mainly because of the growing shortage of nurses. Originally the hospitals were manned by nuns and Protestant deaconesses, but the church, particularly the Evangelical church, has not given its sisterhoods the kind of support that they deserve. One major reason for the decrease in vocations to nursing is the trend towards earlier marriages, and deaconesses who have chosen the path of celibacy may be the answer to this crisis. It should also be recognized that nuns and deaconesses who practically donate their services could enable the modern hospital to remain financially solvent in a time when hospital costs are spiraling. The original deaconess movement is largely a product of Lutheran and Reformed Pietism.

Another para-parochial form of Christian service is the mission house or training institute for missions. We should also mention in this connection the missionary society which sponsors such institutes. In Protestantism the mission houses are the product of the Pietist and Evangelical awakenings. Some of the best-known societies for foreign missions have been the Leipzig mission, the Basel mission and the China Inland Mission. A noted center for the inner mission, i.e., missionary activity in Christian countries, is the St. Chrischona Pilgrim Mission in Basel, Switzerland. This lighthouse, which still exists, comprises a Bible training school for girls, a training institute for laymen or brothers, and a deaconess house. Most of the Bible institutes that have been founded in our country seek to train laymen for both the foreign and inner missions.

A question can be raised as to whether the church today needs mission houses and Bible institutes. We now have hundreds of church-related colleges and many accredited theological seminaries which are open to laymen as well as ministerial students. In addition there are a growing number of special schools for laymen sponsored by seminaries. It is our view that the need for the mission house is greater now than ever primarily because the colleges and seminaries have become much too acclimated to the culture to be able to exert a real influence upon the culture. Our church-related colleges were originally founded for the purpose of training for the Christian apostolate. But in order to maintain academic respectability and also to win the confidence

of the surrounding community they have generally been compelled to compromise even beyond the point of no return. That
not all church colleges have surrendered to secularism and that
secularization has also brought about some gains must not blind
us to the fact that the Christian witness is considerably curtailed
at many of these schools. The present dependence of the colleges
on federal funds has placed a further restriction upon their
witness to the Christian revelation. Our seminaries generally no
longer speak of prayer and evangelism but only of academic
excellence and social relevance. The goals of piety and evangelical zeal have been supplanted by the desire for academic
and cultural prestige. Therefore dedicated Christian laymen
as well as theological students who desire to prepare for a life
of consecrated service and witness need to look beyond the
purely academic institution to centers of evangelical witness
where they can be trained in the life of the spirit.

The hospitality house should also be considered a live option
for the concerned Christian in our day. By this is meant a
house or center which provides hospitality and refuge for the
homeless, the very poor, the despised or those in special
need. Teen Challenge, which receives support from Pentecostal
churches, sponsors such houses for drug addicts. The Catholic
Worker movement has established hospitality houses for tran-
sients in the slums of New York.[11] Some churches are sponsoring
halfway houses for ex-convicts and also for alcoholics in order
to help them readjust to society.

When the secular theologians speak of para-parochial forms
of church life, they usually have in mind groups that are centered about social action. There is a place for such organizations
in the church so long as they seek to bring the Word of God
and not simply the latest findings of sociology to bear upon the
critical issues of our time. Moreover, the issues that they should
be concerned with are not those of a partisan political nature
but spiritual issues — where obedience to God is at stake.
Such issues today would be the racial crisis, the threat of nuclear war, the population explosion and the breakdown in sexual mores. The means that social action groups employ should
be consonant with the Christian mission, and this might entail
nonviolent resistance but not the use of force. Saul Alinsky,
who contends that any means justifies the end, is not the proper
guide for Christians in this area. Examples of extra-ecclesiastical

11 See Ethel Gintoft, "Hospitality House in Milwaukee," *Catholic Digest*,
Vol. 32, No. 7 (May, 1968), pp. 17-19.

organizations of a social or political nature are the worker priests in France, the Fellowship of Reconciliation, the Catholic Interracial Council, and Martin Luther King's Southern Christian Leadership Conference.

Among the most exciting ventures in Christian mission are the new kinds of religious communities that have developed within the past several decades in both Protestantism and Roman Catholicism. The religious community or religious order as a form of special consecration has deep roots in the Christian tradition.[12] In the early church we need think only of the Parabolani, a lay order devoted to the care of the sick, the community of widows mentioned by the apostle (I Tim. 5:9-12) and the coenobitic communities such as the Benedictines and Augustinians. In the medieval church we can point to the Friends of God, the Lollards, the Brethren of the Common Life, and the new orders of friars, the Franciscans and Dominicans. The Evangelical Reformation protested against the religious orders but not because of an aversion to community life but rather because of the theology of works-righteousness which permeated so many of these orders. Religious communities reappeared in Protestant history including the Treveka community in Wales, the Shaker and Amana communities in America, the deaconess communities, the Community of Little Gidding in England, the Herrnhut community of the Moravians in Germany and the Church Army in the Anglican church. Mention should also be made of the Anglo-Catholic communities most of which began in the nineteenth century, although only a very few of these orders are evangelical in orientation.[13] The Roman Catholic church has also seen many new forms of religious life arise in its midst. The most famous modern Catholic order is the Jesuits which seeks to take the monastery out into the world.

Among the radical new experiments in community life in Roman Catholicism today are the Little Brothers of Jesus, who seek to minister in the world in ordinary rather than religious garb; the Order of the Ark in France, a pacifist community including married people; the Focolari, a lay order dedicated to Christian apostolate; the Catholic Worker farms; and the secular institutes (such as the Opus Dei) which give Christian laymen the opportunity to live the counsels of perfection in the world. Mention can also be made of the erosion of many

---

[12] See Frederick D. Leete, *Christian Brotherhoods* (Cincinnati: Jennings & Graham, 1912), pp. 13-19.

[13] See Peter F. Anson, *The Call of the Cloister* (London: S.P.C.K., 1956).

of the established orders as men and women seek a more meaningful expression of their apostolic vocation. The Glenmary Sisters, for example, have been seriously depleted, since a majority of their members have left to live in small groups close to the centers of worldly need. There is a quest in modern Catholicism for a new kind of spirituality, one that is geared more to Christian apostolate in the world than to contemplation.[14] The trend towards a world-directed spirituality can also be seen in Greek Catholicism; for example, we might mention the Zoe Brotherhood in Greece, an order of laymen who seek to witness in the world by preaching and service.

Modern Protestantism has also witnessed the emergence of new forms of community life.[15] Some of these communities are open to married persons as well as single. Among the new lighthouses in Protestantism is the brotherhood of Taizé in France, a community of men who have voluntarily embraced a life of celibacy and poverty in order to be completely free to serve Christ in the world. The Ecumenical Sisterhood of Mary in Darmstadt, Germany, was founded by Klara Schlink after the second world war for the purposes of intercession, retreat and evangelism. The Brotherhood of Christ located in Selbitz, Germany, functions as a double cloister, being open to both men and women who pledge themselves to celibacy and a community of goods. It was founded by Pastor Walter Hümmer and his wife, both spiritually gifted persons; the core of the community is the young people's fellowship of their former parish.[16] The Lee Abbey community in Devonshire, England, is composed of both single and married persons who organize house parties for guests as a kind of fellowship evangelism. The Company of the Cross in Selkirk, Manitoba, an Anglican community, manages a school for boys and is open to both married and single people. Other Protestant communities worthy of notice are the Daughters of Mary in Denmark; the Sisters of Grandchamp in Switzerland; the Agape community in Italy; St. Julian's community in England; the Iona community in Scotland; the community of Imshausen in Germany; the reor-

14 See Jordan Aumann, Donald G. Bloesch, and Thomas Hopko, *Christian Spirituality East and West* (Chicago: Priory Press, 1968).

15 See Donald G. Bloesch, *Centers of Christian Renewal* (Philadelphia: United Church Press, 1964); Olive Wyon, *Living Springs* (Philadelphia: Westminster, 1964); Francois Biot, *The Rise of Protestant Monasticism* (Baltimore: Helicon, 1963); and Siegfried von Kortzfleisch, *Mitten Im Herzen Der Massen* (Stuttgart: Kreuz-Verlag, 1963).

16 Siegfried von Kortzfleisch, *Mitten Im Herzen Der Massen,* pp. 100-109.

ganized Brethren of the Common Life in Germany and Switzerland; and Bethany Fellowship in Minnesota. All of these communities and orders see themselves as special working fellowships within the larger church rather than as sects or utopian communities.[17] They seek to be both evangelical and catholic in that their aim is to hold in balance the evangelical message of free grace and the catholic ideal of the holy life.

There are other new forms of church life that should be mentioned. The Evangelical academies in Germany seek to reach modern secularized man for the Gospel by means of dialogues between the various segments and classes of society.[18] These academies are not quite so strong today as in previous years partly because dialogue by itself is not sufficient to penetrate the secular enclave. The coffee house ministry is another experiment in evangelism, and this form of ministry has much promise. Yet here again when dialogue becomes a substitute for direct witnessing, the possibility of real communication is vitiated. The Salvation Army Coffee House in the Soho district of London is an example of how such an experiment can be successfully operated to the greater glory of God and the furtherance of the kingdom. This coffee house is not simply a place where people can enter for relaxation, refreshments and perhaps meaningful dialogue but also where men and women are challenged with the Gospel message of reconciliation. Other extra-ecclesiastical forms of church life are the spiritual renewal movements such as the Disciplined Order of Christ and Camps Farthest Out, the student evangelism fellowships like Campus Crusade for Christ and the Inter-Varsity Christian Fellowship and such independent evangelistic fellowships as the Navigators, which actually functions as a Protestant religious order.

Harvey Cox has stated that the real ecumenical crisis today is not between Catholics and Protestants but between traditional and experimental forms of church life.[19] John Robinson con-

17 Many of the communities in Protestant history have been utopian and sectarian rather than authentically evangelical and catholic. We have in mind the Shakers, the Icarians, the Amana community, and the House of David. The Moral Re-Armament community at Caux, Switzerland, is shaped much more by a syncretistic mysticism than by an evangelical piety. The Society of Brothers (the Bruderhof) contains evangelical as well as utopian, sectarian motifs. Its founder Eberhard Arnold warned against confusing community life with the church of Christ itself, and thereby he helped to prevent his movement from becoming only another sect.

18 See Lee J. Gable, *Church and World Encounter* (Philadelphia: United Church Press, 1964).

19 Harvey Cox, *The Secular City* (N.Y.: Macmillan, 1965), p. 160.

tends that the hope of the church lies in experimental and exploratory ministries.[20] We share these views but at the same time hold that the new ministries must be seen not simply as means to the service of man but to the service of the evangelical proclamation. Communities such as the Ecumenical Institute in Chicago and the now defunct Parishfield community in Michigan do not represent our ideal in community life, since it is a secular gospel and not the biblical gospel that forms the content of their witness.[21]

### THE CHURCH'S HIDDEN POTENTIAL

In a discussion of new forms of church life we can gain some understanding of the hidden potential of the church. One of the untapped resources in our Protestant churches is the single woman, who is very much overlooked.[22] Such women might rediscover their vocation if they were given an opportunity to enter a community of women like St. Julian's or the Sisters of Mary or a mixed community like the Church Army or Lee Abbey. Deaconess communities such as Riehen and Kaiserswerth should also be given serious consideration.[23] The only role generally open to the woman has been that of housewife and mother, but the Christian vocation is one of apostolate, and all Christians should be encouraged in this direction. This is not to minimize the blessings of marriage and family, but it is to affirm that even the married woman has a vocation to Christian service and mission and her family duties do not exhaust this vocation. The Roman Catholic church has made a real place for the single woman in the area of *diakonia* (Christian service), but it has overlooked the married woman. In this time of runaway population, the church should encourage small families, families that would have the freedom to serve and work beyond the family setting. A word should also be said about the childless couple, another neglected party in the church. Such persons are generally encouraged to adopt children rather than to give

---

20 John Robinson, *The New Reformation?*, pp. 96f.

21 See Arthur McNally, "Religion For A One-Story Universe" in *The Sign* (Jan., 1968), Vol. 47, No. 6, pp. 30-34. Also see "Church Funds for Revolution" in *Christianity Today* (April 26, 1968), pp. 27, 28.

22 See Kathleen Bliss, *The Service and Status of Women in the Churches* (London: SCM, 1954); and A. M. Carré, *The Vocation of the Single Woman*, trans. Una Morrissy (N.Y.: P. J. Kenedy, 1960).

23 For a penetrating appraisal of the modern deaconess movement see *The Deaconess: A Service of Women in the World Today* (Geneva: World Council of Churches, 1966).

themselves to the missionary apostolate. Couples in this position could very profitably be used on the mission field or in inner city missions where couples with children would be at a distinct disadvantage. The single man even more than the single woman has been ignored in the modern church, particularly in Protestantism. There is a place for the celibate life for both men and women, and the advantages of this kind of life in certain kinds of missionary and charitable work should not be underestimated.[24] It is well to remember that the early Methodist Circuit Riders were nearly all single men and that Bishop Asbury strongly recommended celibacy for the itinerant evangelist.

Another group within the church that could be profitably tapped for full-time church service are the elderly. In this category we find many people who are free of family responsibilities and who would be most ready to devote the remaining years of their life to Christian service. We have in mind here widows and widowers, bachelors and spinsters, couples whose children have left home, and those who are divorced or separated. Many of these people could be colporteurs, secretaries in church offices, or sisters and brothers of mercy who visit prisoners, the mentally ill and the physically sick. We should also not close our eyes to the silent ministry of intercessory prayer which entails time as well as concentration. But who has this time more than our elderly?

In this same connection much more attention needs to be given by the church to its retired ministers and teachers of religion. Here are men and women who have dedicated a lifetime to the ministry of preaching and teaching, and yet who in their later years are left without an opportunity of using their accumulated wisdom in the service of the church. Retired ministers could be profitably employed by larger churches in the areas of counseling, Sunday School teaching and/or visitation. Those clergymen who are financially self-supporting might be encouraged to give spiritual direction at retreat centers and hospitality houses.

In the next chapter we intend to explore another side of Christian life that has been very much neglected in mainstream

---

24 At the annual assembly of the National Council of Churches' Division of Foreign Missions in Buck Hill Falls, Pa. (1962) Dr. Gwenyth Hubble, a World Council of Churches executive whose specialty is training missionary personnel, suggested that future Protestant missionaries could be more effective if they remained unmarried, at least for a limited time. See *The Presbyterian Outlook*, Vol. 144, No. 46 (Dec. 17, 1962), pp. 3, 4.

Protestantism: the charismatic gifts. Out of a rediscovery of the gifts of the Spirit may come a deeper appreciation for new kinds of ministry and new forms of church life. Perhaps the one resource that the church needs most to rediscover is the Holy Spirit, since only the Spirit can create new forms of permanent value and only the Spirit can enliven and remold old forms of church life.

# NINE:

# THE CHARISMATIC GIFTS

### TYPES OF CHARISMS

The Pentecostal and neo-Pentecostal revivals have focused attention once again upon the gifts of the Spirit. The older Protestant orthodoxy held that the extraordinary charisms disappeared with the apostolic age, but this view is now being seriously questioned. Dr. Edmund Schlink voices the new mood when he declares that "the charismata belong to the essence of the church of all times and of all places."[1] Perhaps the third-force Protestants (esp. the Pentecostals) will move the historic churches to re-examine their position on this matter and arrive at a new understanding and appreciation of the charisms of the Spirit.

A charism (from the Greek *charisma*) signifies a special gift or power which enables one to perform a particular service. The charisms were given by the Spirit primarily for the upbuilding of the church. Every person who is baptized by the Spirit into the body of Christ is also endowed with special gifts or charisms. This is to say, the Christian not only receives the Spirit in faith but also is given particular graces either at the time of his baptism and conversion or subsequently.

Scripture tells us that besides the charisms, there are more general spiritual graces granted to all members of the church enabling them to fulfill their vocation and draw closer to God. Some scholars have seen these gifts exemplified to a superlative degree in the Messiah of Israel (Is. 11:1-3). All believers are called and empowered to share in the ministry of faith and prayer. In Roman Catholic tradition these general graces have been called "the gifts of the Spirit," and they are believed to be bestowed at confirmation. Our position is that the universal gifts (among which we include piety, fortitude, fear of the Lord, faith, hope, and love) are the possession of every believer. In-deed, apart from these gifts we do not have the Spirit.

In addition to the general graces, however, there are special

---

[1] Quoted in *Trinity* (Eastertide, 1963), p. 27.

graces or charisms each of which is given only to some Christians. These are gifts that one has not simply by virtue of belonging to the body of Christ but mainly for the purpose of implementing a specific task in this body. They are potentialities that are created, aroused and appealed to by the Holy Spirit (Küng). They are dispensed not on the basis of personal holiness or merit but rather on the basis of God's plan for each individual life and His church. In Hebrews we are told that the gifts of the Spirit are distributed according to God's own will (2:4). Every Christian is granted some special charism (I Cor. 7:7), but no Christian is a recipient of all the charisms. Paul contends that there is a diversity of gifts and ministries (I Cor. 12:4-6, 11, 28-31), and this truth must not be obscured. In Pentecostal churches it is commonly asserted that there are twelve charisms of the Spirit, but Paul lists altogether at least twenty such gifts (cf. Rom. 12:6-8; I Cor. 12:8-10, 28-30; Eph. 4:11-16). Moreover, in the history of the church many more special charisms have been disclosed, and the church should therefore take care in imposing a limitation on the gifts of the Spirit.

The Constitution on the Church of the Second Vatican Council reaffirms a traditional Catholic distinction between ordinary and extraordinary charisms (I, 12). Without mentioning the charisms by name, it avers that the extraordinary charisms should not be rashly sought after and that judgment as to their authenticity belongs to those who preside over the church. This distinction that Catholic theology makes is helpful, but our view is that the Christian should be open to any gift that will build up the church even though it might be exceptional or extraordinary. He should earnestly desire, however, only the higher gifts (I Cor. 12:31).

The extraordinary charisms of the Spirit might be considered preternatural gifts in that they point beyond but do not necessarily transcend the natural order. Among these are divine healing, the working of miracles, prophecy, wonder-working faith, the discerning of spirits, speaking in tongues and the interpretation of tongues (I Cor. 12). We might also include mystical visions, immunity to poison, demon exorcism, the reading of hearts, pneumatic wisdom and preternatural knowledge.[2] Ex-

---

2 Fathers Aumann and Royo classify extraordinary gifts under *gratiae gratis datae* (gratuitous graces). They include in this category such phenomena as visions, locutions, private revelations, the reading of hearts, the working of miracles, inedia or absolute fasting, stigmata, prophecy, healing,

traordinary gifts were foretold by the prophet Joel (2:28) and also promised by Christ (Mk. 16:17, 18).

Extraordinary charisms are very much in evidence in biblical history. In the Old Testament Abraham can be said to have had the charism of discerning of spirits, Moses the charism to work miracles, Joseph the gifts of knowledge and prophecy, both Job and Solomon the gift of wisdom, Elijah the charisms of prophecy, healing and miracles, and Daniel the gifts of knowledge, prophecy and the interpretation of tongues. Isaiah, Jeremiah, Ezekiel and indeed all of the prophets can be considered charismatic figures. In the New Testament Jesus was endowed with many special charisms including healing, the discerning of spirits, the working of miracles, demon exorcism, the reading of hearts and prophecy. His disciples also manifested the working of the Spirit in their healings, preachings, and exorcisms. Charisms that Paul possessed at one time or another during his ministry were healing, prophecy, exorcism, the discerning of spirits, immunity to poison, and very probably tongues.

Among those in the New Testament church who seemed to have a particular vocation to prophecy were Agabus, Judas, Silas and the four daughters of Philip (Ac. 11:28; 21:10; 15:32; 21:9). It appears that these and others who were similarly gifted journeyed from place to place strengthening their brethren in the faith; they were said to rank in importance next to the apostles (I Cor. 12:28; Eph. 2:20; 3:5; 4:11). As in the case of the Old Testament prophets their utterances contained comparatively little definite prediction, although this note was not absent (Ac. 11:28; 21:10). What characterized their prophecies was a searching appeal that awakened the conscience and edified the soul.

Other gifts that are somewhat less spectacular but that can still be considered extraordinary are preaching, teaching, evangelism and spiritual writing. It is well to note that Paul places both preaching and teaching before the gift of tongues (I Cor. 12:28). The apostle also mentions charisms that are more widespread and therefore are not to be considered exceptional: exhortation and acts of mercy (Rom. 12:8), service (Rom. 12:7), and helping and administration (I Cor. 12:28). Several of these gifts depending on how they are used might also partake of

---

levitation, mystical aureoles, bodily elongation and tongues. See Antonio Royo and Jordan Aumann, *The Theology of Christian Perfection* (Dubuque: Priory Press, 1962), pp. 639f. It should be recognized that many of these gifts are simply variations of more fundamental gifts.

the extraordinary. Both our Lord and the apostle Paul speak of celibacy and marriage as also being gifts of the Spirit, and this is something that should be emphasized today particularly when celibacy is under a cloud and marriage is often reduced to a purely biological transaction.

## THE CHARISMS IN HISTORICAL PERSPECTIVE

Most church historians agree that the apostolic church was a charismatic, spiritual fellowship. Special charisms were very much in evidence, and Paul even had to caution against their misuse (I Cor. 13, 14). Free prayer was quite common in the services of worship, and personal testimonies were very much in order. By the second century, however, church services became much more formal, and the sacraments loomed very significant. The Montanist movement in the second and third centuries signalized a reaction against growing formalism and sacramentalism with a pronounced emphasis upon the outpouring of the Spirit, the charismatic gifts, new revelations and the imminent end of the world. Tertullian after becoming a Montanist made a distinction between the "psychics," those who live by animal standards, and the "pneumatics," those who were filled with the Spirit. The church historian Harnack maintains that the Montanists recovered the spiritual vigor and spontaneity of the New Testament church, although we should also point out that the movement from the beginning was imperiled by legalism and moralism.

Medieval Roman Catholicism made a place for mystics, eccentrics and charismatics, but it was not kindly disposed towards prophets and reformers. It allowed for extraordinary spiritual gifts but refused to accept the authenticity of such gifts until it was proved that the doctrine of the one so inspired conformed to canon law and Holy Writ. Thomas Aquinas held that charisms are not dependent on the holiness of the recipient and are given for the good of the community. For the most part in Roman Catholic history extraordinary charisms are associated with the great saints and mystics. One of the hallmarks of the saint is the working of miracles. Visions and mystical ecstasy, too, are seen as manifestations of sainthood. The stigmata, the bodily marks resembling the wounds of the crucified Christ, are also generally valued as evidences of sanctity. Speaking in tongues is accepted in Roman Catholic theology, but for the most part tongues have been regarded as an existing rather than an ecstatic language. Vincent Ferrer is reputed to have had this particular gift among many others. Catholic theologians often distinguish between charism and office and charism and rite. There can be an office of exorcism and a charism of exorcism. There is the sacrament of healing, viz., extreme unction, and a charism of healing.

The Protestant Reformation was marked by a profound distrust of visions, bizarre gifts, healings and indeed anything that smacked of superstition and magic. Luther and Calvin were insistent that the Christian walk by faith alone and not rely upon signs and wonders. They acknowledged the miracles and healings of the New Testament but maintained that such phenomena ceased with the close of the apostolic age. Karl Barth in our day reflects this emphasis of the Reformation in his belief that the miracles of Jesus are absolutely unique. The Reformers allowed for the special anointing of the Spirit for the purposes of preaching and teaching but not for healings, tongues or miracles. They made a place for the charism of celibacy but regarded it as very exceptional. Marriage in their view was not a spiritual grace but belonged wholly to the order of nature. The Reformation rediscovered the gift of charismatic preaching, but the charismata as such were disregarded.

The charismatic gifts began to reappear in left-wing and revivalistic Protestantism. Prophecy and glossolalia were present among some of the Anabaptists. George Fox, the founder of the Quakers, was a charismatic personality and was blessed with various preternatural gifts including mystical visions, the discerning of spirits, healing and prophecy.[3] The movements of Pietism and Evangelicalism further focused attention upon the workings and gifts of the Holy Spirit. Johann Christoph Blumhardt, the noted Pietist theologian, was not only a gifted preacher but also a noted healer and exorcist. Johann Frederick Rock and Christian Metz were regarded by the Community of True Inspiration (Amana community) as latter-day prophets. In the radical Evangelical or Holiness movement, which emerged in the nineteenth century, the gift of the Spirit was associated with a second crisis experience after conversion, but charismatic phenomena were generally viewed with suspicion. The charisms of the Spirit were particularly prevalent among sect groups such as the Shakers, the Mormons, the Irvingites and the Christian Catholics (Doweyites). All these groups, like the early Montanists, stressed the latter-day outpouring of the Spirit and

---

3 See Henry J. Cadbury, ed., *George Fox's Book of Miracles* (Cambridge: University Press, 1948).

the proliferation of charismatic gifts. Among the charisms that were stressed in one or other of these sects were prophecy, private revelations, the working of miracles, tongues and healing. Seventh Day Adventists, who also stand in continuity with Montanism, have placed a pronounced emphasis upon prophecy, the discerning of spirits and private revelations. Emanuel Swedenborg, who had a great influence upon the Spiritualists as well as upon the movement that bears his name, was a noted mystic and clairvoyant who while in England accurately described the great fire in Stockholm, how it occurred and when it was extinguished.

In the twentieth century the charisms of the Spirit have been given prominence in the Pentecostal movement, which is partly an offshoot of the Holiness revival. The distinctive mark of Pentecostalism is the belief that tongues are an evidential or confirmatory sign of the baptism of the Spirit which, as in Holiness theology, is equated with a crisis experience subsequent to conversion. The gifts of the Spirit are also stressed in such interdenominational spiritual renewal movements as Camps Farthest Out and the Spiritual Frontiers Fellowship as well as in religious communities like the Ecumenical Sisterhood of Mary and the reorganized Brethren of the Common Life. The New Apostolic Church, which is the largest of the sects in Germany today, has also made a place for the charisms of the Spirit including prophecy, tongues and the discerning of spirits.

## TOWARD THE RECOVERY OF THE CHARISMATIC GIFTS

If we are to have spiritual renewal in our time, the church must be open again to the special gifts and charisms given by the Spirit of God for the purpose of ministry in the world. Such gifts must not be regarded as evidence of holiness or sanctity nor should they be viewed as signs or proofs of the infilling of the Spirit. We are well aware of the fact that many persons who have been both immoral and flagrantly heretical have nevertheless been endowed with special gifts that can only be regarded as preternatural. Yet when these gifts are in the hands of those who stand solidly on the Scriptural revelation and who seek to use them in the service of Christ, they can be of immense aid to the church in its ministry of reconciliation and redemption. Christianity is after all not only an institutional religion but also a charismatic religion. It is not only a religion of the Word and sacraments but also a religion of the Spirit. Dr. James Luther Adams has contended that "a church that today makes no room for charisma does not stand in continuity with the early ecclesia." Too often we think of miracles and healings as something that belong to a bygone age, but Jesus Himself said that His followers would do even greater works than He did (Jn. 14:12).

Speaking in tongues can be accepted as a gift of the Spirit, but it should not be regarded as a rational sign or evidence of having the Spirit. It may be a manifestation of the Spirit particularly if joy, love and faith are present, but the heathen also can be moved in this way (I Cor. 12:2). Some Pentecostal churches are now recognizing that the Spirit can be given apart from tongues and that tongues may be present even where the Spirit is absent.[4] Tongue-speech is neither gibberish nor a foreign language (although it might include foreign words) but rather an ecstatic language, a language emanating from the unconscious.[5] Glossolalia is an automatism similar to automatic writing, spirit dancing and uncontrollable laughter, in which the unconscious takes control of the personality. (This is not to discount the possibility that the Spirit of God may be working in and through the unconscious.) It might also be regarded as a type of somnambulism in which the subject is detached from his immediate surroundings (Kelsey). St. Paul seems to indicate that it is a kind of prayer in that the tongue-speaker addresses not man but God (I Cor. 14:2, 14); yet it should not be seen as true prayer nor a higher form of prayer, since prayer being conversation with God entails both the spirit and the understanding. Tongues, we are told, are given for the purpose of personal edification and therefore benefit the church only indirectly. According to the apostle tongues are neither to be encouraged nor prohibited. They can be seen as sometimes helpful to children in the faith, but when we press on to ma-

---

[4] At the European Pentecostal conference in Stockholm in 1939 it was admitted that tongues might occur apart from the Spirit's action and that one could be filled with the Spirit without the sign of tongues. See M. James, *I Believe in the Holy Ghost* (Minneapolis: Bethany Fellowship, 1965), p. 115.

[5] The phenomenon of speaking an actual language which one previously did not know is better referred to as polyglossia rather than glossolalia which is basically ecstatic utterance. For the current discussion on speaking in tongues see Donald G. Bloesch, "The Charismatic Revival" in *Religion in Life* (Summer, 1966), pp. 364-380; Anthony Hoekema, *What About Tongue Speaking?* (Grand Rapids: Eerdmans, 1966); Frank Staff, E. Glen Hinson and Wayne Oates, *Glossolalia* (Nashville: Abingdon, 1967); Morton T. Kelsey, *Tongue Speaking* (N.Y.: Doubleday, 1964); D. W. Burdick, *Tongues: To Speak or Not to Speak* (Chicago: Moody, 1969); and J. L. Sherrill, *They Speak with Other Tongues* (N.Y.: McGraw-Hill, 1964).

turity they can be set aside (I Cor. 13:8, 11, 13). Tongues are a stepping stone to the gifts that build up the body of Christ such as preaching, teaching, prophecy and above all love.

Yet this is not to underestimate the fact that glossolalia can be of some value to those who have broken through the prison of self-will to saving faith and who are struggling towards deeper personal integration. Speaking in tongues is a crutch or psychic aid that can occasionally benefit even some who are more spiritually advanced, although it more appropriately belongs to the childhood of faith. It can be regarded as a prayer gift that if used properly can strengthen one's communion with God. It enables one to give voice to concerns that have not yet been conceptualized. In Tournier's opinion the gift of tongues served to deepen the fellowship and spirituality of the apostolic church.[6] St. Paul cautioned against the use of tongues in services of public worship (I Cor. 14:23-25, 34-36), but he certainly sanctioned it in small prayer groups and private devotions. Tongues can edify the inner man, but they are a sign of scandal to those outside the faith (I Cor. 14:22). Cullmann maintains that in the New Testament speaking in tongues has eschatological significance, since it foreshadows the future angelic language;[7] yet this can be disputed in the light of Paul's testimony that tongues will pass away, whereas faith, hope and love have permanent validity (I Cor. 13:8f.).

Our objection to the Pentecostals is that they tend to view tongues as the evidential sign of the baptism of the Spirit or (as it is sometimes called) the experience of entire sanctification.[8] The seeking for tongues can too often become a craving after signs (as in some tarrying services), and faith is then supplanted by sight. In Reformed theology the Christian receives the Spirit in baptism and faith. All Christians are indwelt by the Spirit, but we should also seek to be filled with the Spirit. Yet only by our fruits can we attest that we have

---

[6] Paul Tournier, *The Meaning of Persons*, trans. Edwin Hudson (N.Y.: Harper, 1957), p. 173.

[7] Oscar Cullmann, *Salvation In History* (N.Y.: Harper, 1965), pp. 256, 305, 306.

[8] In the original Pentecostal movement the baptism of the Spirit was either regarded as subsequent to the experience of entire sanctification or was practically equated with this experience. The Pentecostal Holiness church reflects this emphasis, for it speaks of three distinct experiences — conversion, entire sanctification and Spirit-baptism. Many Pentecostal churches, however, no longer hold to a correlation between Spirit-baptism and total sanctification. The Assemblies of God, the largest Pentecostal body in America, adheres to the doctrine of progressive sanctification.

the Spirit. Some Pentecostals such as Karl Schneider acknowledge that glossolalia can also be a work of the flesh, and that
the decisive mark of being in the Spirit is inner peace and joy.

The Reformed theologian Hendrikus Berkhof holds that the
gift of prophecy should again be emphasized, since the church
needs to hear a sure word concerning the will of God in the
precarious times in which we live.[9] Prophecy does not necessarily mean the prediction of future events, but it does mean the
ability to discern the hand of God at work in the present and
to understand what God would have us do both now and in
the future. Prophecy is both "forth-telling" and foretelling, but
the latter must grow out of the former. There have been some
notable personalities who have given prophetic counsel in our
time, e.g., Jeane Dixon and Edgar Cayce, but their counsel
must be tested in the light of Scripture to determine whether
it indeed comes from God (I Jn. 4:1). Even if some prophecies
are proved to be uncannily correct, they may have their source
in the diabolical rather than the divine. In our estimation P.
T. Forsyth was an authentic prophet, since he accurately discerned the spiritual crisis which was only then beginning to
shake the English church and indeed western Christendom.
Moreover, he brought the Word of God to bear upon this
crisis by calling his church to repentance and radical reformation.

A fascination with prophecy can be a danger in the church
particularly when it is regarded as a direct revelation from God
rather than an indirect disclosure of the will of God through
meditation upon Scripture. Too often prophecies are seen as
new revelations which are placed on the same level as the
biblical revelation. In some churches that have been influenced
by the charismatic revival, prophecy is given more prominence
than the sermon, and occasionally the sermons are based upon
the latest prophecy rather than upon Scripture. It is our recommendation that prophecies not be uttered in the services of worship and that they generally be given only at special meetings
or in semi-private gatherings so that they can be tested in the
light of Scripture before being publicized. True prophecies
are informed by Scripture and spring out of costly discipleship
to Christ; being solidly anchored in Scripture and the Christian
life they are practically self-authenticating.

What we have called pneumatic wisdom is surely another
charism that can be a great blessing to the church. The charism

---

[9] Hendrikus Berkhof, *The Doctrine of the Holy Spirit* (Richmond: John
Knox, 1964), pp. 91, 92.

of wisdom should be distinguished from natural sagacity which may be a genuine divine endowment, but it is not a charismatic gift. It is well to note that Paul speaks of the "utterance of wisdom" *(logos sophias)*, which means that this gift has a social character. It is intended to be expressed for the benefit of others or for the good of the church at large. The word of wisdom is not attained by education but is given by the Holy Spirit; therefore the glory belongs to God and not to man. It can be exercised at a critical juncture in church affairs, as, e.g., in Ac. 15 where James (who was inclined to be a legalist) states that the Gentiles should not be given the added burden of circumcision but rather should be asked to abstain from idols and unchastity (vss. 19, 20). It can also be exercised profitably in both pastoral counseling and personal witnessing. Too often pastors seek to draw upon their knowledge of psychology in dealing with souls in torment, whereas what is needed is a word of spiritual wisdom that is available to them if they would only seek it.

Demon exorcism is certainly a crying need in our time, since the main problem today is one of bondage. Moreover, we should understand this bondage as being not merely to psychological or sociological forces but to principalities and powers that enter this world from the beyond. In contradistinction again to many Pentecostalists we do not interpret the demons in the animistic sense, i.e., as discarnate spirits wandering about in the air seeking bodies to inhabit. But in opposition to the demythologizers we also believe that it is a mistake to understand the demons as subterranean psychological forces. Rather they should be viewed as transhistorical powers with mind and purpose that seek to bend the will of man in the direction of radical evil. More will be said about the nature of demons and exorcism in the next chapter.

The charism of the discerning of spirits is very necessary in our day when pagan cults and alien ideologies are making a bid for the souls of men. Very few German Christians recognized the demonic character of Nazism and if it had not been for the witness of the confessing church in Germany the Nazi triumph would have been complete in that country. Many Christians today are blind to the diabolical nature of Communism and the new nationalisms. Some theologians seem unable to discern the insidious character of the Playboy philosophy and in an eagerness to come to terms with this philosophy have practically abandoned the precepts of their faith. Jesus warned against false

prophets that would appear in the latter days (Mt. 24:11, 24).
We need today spiritually gifted men and women who can discriminate between truth and error, the divine and the demonic.
The discernment of the depths of one's afflictions (which we
have called the reading of hearts) might be regarded as one
aspect or manifestation of this gift, and this kind of spiritual
diagnosis is also needed in our time.[10]

Spiritual healing is a charism that should be encouraged for
those who feel themselves gifted in this direction. The healing
ministry has for the most part been taken over by the small sects
and cults, and the church needs to recover this dimension of
its mission. It is nevertheless imperative that a distinction be
made between divine healing and magical healing by which
one seeks to bring about the desired result through special procedures and techniques. The gift of healing like other spiritual
gifts is not an accomplishment that we can take pride in but
rather a manifestation of the power of Christ's Spirit in and
through us.

Charismatic preaching is also sorely needed in our time. When
theologians are speaking about a famine of the Word of God,
we need to hear this word proclaimed by Spirit-filled men. Paul
wrote that his message was not in plausible words of wisdom
"but in demonstration of the Spirit and power" (I Cor. 2:4).
One of the hallmarks of charismatic preaching is boldness (par-
rēsia) (Ac. 4:13, 29, 31). Neither professional training in speech
nor theological study can by themselves enable one to preach
the word of God with power and authority. This is a gift for
which every ordained clergyman, theological student and lay
preacher should earnestly pray and seek.

Perhaps more attention should be given to the charism of
founding and supervising institutions. In the nineteenth century
such pioneering spirits as Friedrich Bodelschwingh, John Bost,
Georges Appia and Christian Spittler were instrumental in the
founding of new institutions devoted to Christian mission and
service to the downtrodden and forsaken. Among these institutions were deaconess houses, epileptic homes, asylums for the
mentally retarded, rest homes for the emotionally distraught
and centers for lay evangelism. This kind of charism is related
to the gift of administration, which Paul places before tongues
(see I Cor. 12:28). There is a need today for men and women

---

10 The reading of hearts might also be considered a variant of the charism
of preternatural knowledge.

with vision and foresight who will organize and direct new forms of Christian ministry.

Hans Küng reminds us that teaching is also a charism of the Spirit and that the church needs to pay heed to its teachers or theologians.[11] A church that ignores its theologians is obstructing the work of the Spirit, for the Spirit's task is to purify and reformulate the doctrine of the church as well as to empower for missionary proclamation. A theologian to be sure is only a charismatic figure if he combines intellectual acumen and prayer, research and adoration. He must write and teach not only out of fidelity to the Word but also in the power of the Spirit if he is to be considered a trustworthy spiritual guide. Unlike the prophet who speaks intuitively to a particular situation, the teacher gives a systematic exposition of the truth of faith.

Every Christian is in one sense a charismatic personality, since those who truly believe are indwelt by the Holy Spirit. Every believer should radiate the power of the Spirit and manifest the fruits of the Spirit. Every member of the body of Christ is a beneficiary of at least some charism or grace that equips him for kingdom service. Yet only a relatively few are gifted with extraordinary charisms and therefore can be regarded as charismatic figures in the special sense. Such charisms may be a curse rather than a blessing if they are not rightly used. Although they may connote greater responsibility, they do not necessarily indicate deeper communion with the Spirit.

The modern era has been blessed with many notable charismatic figures, contrary to what is commonly believed. We might mention the French priest Jean Vianney (d. 1859) who through his prayers and exorcisms healed thousands of people who were crippled spiritually and physically.[12] He is also credited with the miracle of the multiplication of food. Sadhu Sundar Singh, the Hindu who was converted to evangelical Christianity in the early part of this century, had many extraordinary gifts including the working of miracles, immunity to poison, and interior as well as external visions.[13] He is reputed even to have been

---

11 See Hans Küng, *The Church* (N.Y.: Sheed & Ward, 1967), pp. 396, 397.

12 See Henri Ghéon, *The Secret of the Curé D' Ars,* trans. F. J. Sheed (London: Longmans, Green, 1929).

13 See B. H. Streeter and A. J. Appasamy, *The Message of Sadhu Sundar Singh* (N.Y.: Macmillan, 1922); and A. J. Appasamy, ed., *The Cross In Heaven: The Life and Writings of Sadhu Sundar Singh* (N.Y.: Association, 1957). Other Protestant theologians who have given an appreciative appraisal of Sundar Singh are N. Söderblom and F. Heiler. Catholic theologians who

been caught up into Paradise and to have had communion with the saints as did Christ on the Mount of Transfiguration. Like the great majority of Catholic mystics the Sadhu cautioned against the seeking after supernatural gifts and visions, since this can open one to the incursion of demons. Even many critics of Dr. Billy Graham have been compelled to acknowledge that he has the charism of evangelistic preaching which has been a means of salvation to countless thousands. Frank Buchman, the founder of the Oxford Group movement, had the extraordinary gift of reading hearts and thereby was able to tell what was troubling a person even on a first meeting.[14] His diagnoses were almost invariably correct, although his prescriptions sometimes left something to be desired. Agnes Sanford, noted author and healer, has been instrumental in the healing of untold numbers, and many of her cures have been of maladies that were deemed incurable.[15] The Quaker mystic Hannah Hurnard has had the gifts of prophecy, visions, and healing.[16] William Branham, a Pentecostal preacher, was empowered to discern spirits and read hearts as well as heal; he used the former gifts to diagnose the nature of the ailments of the people who came to him.[17] Mother Basilea Schlink, the founder of the Ecumenical Sisterhood of Mary, has been blessed with numerous charisms including healing, prophecy, the discerning of spirits, the working of miracles and tongues.[18] She is a gifted as well as a holy

---

have praised the Sadhu include Delahaye, de Grandmaison, von Hügel and K. Adam. The claims of Sundar Singh have been disputed by the Catholics H. Hosten and G. Schulemann and the Protestant scholar P. Pfister.

[14] See Peter Howard, *Frank Buchman's Secret* (London: Heinemann, 1961).

[15] Among her books are *The Healing Light* (St. Paul: Macalester Park Publishing Co., 1961); *Behold Your God* (Macalester Park Publishing Co., 1958); and *The Healing Gifts of the Spirit* (Philadelphia: Lippincott, 1966).

[16] See Hannah Hurnard, *Dr. Luke's Clinic* (London: Olive Press, 1961); *The Secrets of the Kingdom* (Olive Press, 1959); *The Keys of the Kingdom* (Olive Press, n.d.).

[17] Among other preternatural gifts and blessings that this very humble Christian pastor has reputedly been given are the working of miracles, the foretelling of the future, angelic visitations and a mystical aureola. It is well to note that Branham is not sectarian, for he has earnestly sought and prayed for the unity of the church. For his amazing story see Gordon Lindsay, *William Branham — A Man Sent From God* (1950), and Julius Stadsklev, *William Branham, A Prophet Visits South Africa* (1952).

[18] See Mother Basilea Schlink, *God Is Always Greater*, trans. N. B. Cryer, foreword by Olive Wyon (London: Faith Press, 1963); and her *Realities*, trans. Larry Christenson and William Castell (Grand Rapids: Zondervan, 1966).

woman, and her writings will surely take a place among the mystical literature of all ages.

The radically charismatic figure will always signify a deviation from the cultural norm. More often than not such persons manifest a deeper sensitivity to the things of the spirit. Unless they also have the gift of wisdom, however, they are prone to place a wrong interpretation upon their gifts. The Christian should not be encouraged to seek for the more spectacular charisms, since such gifts can readily be misused particularly by those who are still only children in the faith. On the other hand, if one feels that he is being prompted by the Spirit in a particular direction, he should probably pursue this path provided that there is reason to believe that he could make a solid contribution to the upbuilding of the church and the extension of the kingdom.

Protestantism ideally should be a coat of many colors. But particularly in the past few decades it has become more like a grey flannel suit. The recent tendency in ecumenical circles to view every Christian as a minister obscures the special nature of the charismatic ministries. If all are healers, then one may be led to assume that there is no special gift of healing or no special ministry of healing. According to Paul there is a diversity of gifts and ministries. He makes very clear that not all possess gifts of healing, prophecy or tongues (I Cor. 12:29-31). Not all Christians can be spiritual directors, pastors or confessors; only some are shepherds and fathers in the faith (I Cor. 4:15).

It is imperative that today there be a renewal of the experience of Pentecost. Nothing less than a new outpouring of the Holy Spirit can give us the illumination and power to reform the church and convert the world. But we must beware of trying to make the experience of the Spirit conform to stereotyped forms. The Spirit works in many ways and He bestows many different gifts. Moreover, special charisms are given even to those who do not know Christ, so we must also be wary of viewing any particular gift as a proof or sign of having the Spirit. The only real evidence of the working of the Spirit lies in the fruits of outgoing love, peace, gentleness, kindness and fidelity (Gal. 5:22). Jesus said that His disciples would be known by their fruits (Mt. 7:16; 12:33), and this is what we must look for in seeking to evaluate the spirituality of any person or movement.

Too often the institutional church has tried to suppress the charismatic element, and thereby it has become ever more barren and sterile. We need to make room for the charismatic element but at the same time channel it in the right direction. Karl Rahner has given these words of wisdom on this subject:

> And so the charismatic element, when it is new, and one might almost say it is only charismatic if it is so, has something shocking about it. It can be mistaken for facile enthusiasm, a hankering after change, attempted subversion, lack of feeling for tradition and the well-tried experience of the past. And precisely those who are firmly rooted in the old, who have preserved a living Christianity as a sacred inheritance from the past, are tempted to extinguish the new spirit, which does not always fix on what is most tried and tested, and yet may be a holy spirit for all that, and to oppose it in the name of the Church's Holy Spirit, although it is a spiritual gift of that Spirit.[19]

The church has always been intolerant of its prophets and only slightly more tolerant of its mystics. Walter Luthi has rightly observed that whenever the fire of the Holy Spirit breaks out, the fire engines of the church authorities are soon there to extinguish it.[20] Let us be open to new movements and experiments in the church so long as they are not palpably heretical. If they are not of God they will soon expire, and if they are, the messianic age may already be upon us (cf. Ac. 5:34f.) .

---

[19] Karl Rahner, *The Dynamic Element in the Church*, trans. W. J. O'Hara (N.Y.: Herder & Herder, 1964), p. 83.

[20] Walter Luthi, *The Letter to the Romans*, trans. Kurt Schoenenberger (Richmond: John Knox, 1961), p. 169.

TEN:

# DIVINE HEALING

## NEED FOR DIVINE HEALING

The twentieth century has witnessed the proliferation of various sects and cults that include healing among their cardinal tenets. We might think here of the Pentecostals, the Christian Scientists, the Unity School of Christianity, the New Thought movement, the Spiritists and many others. Such movements remind those of us who stand in the mainstream of historic Christianity that healing is one of the basic ministries of the church.

Yet healing has been neglected by the modern church, particularly the Protestant church. There are several reasons for this. First one must consider the fact that both Luther and Calvin believed the charism of healing to be restricted to the apostolic age. They rightly pointed to the unique character of the ministry of our Lord, but they seemingly ignored the promise of Jesus that His followers would do greater things than He did (Jn. 14:12). Again, the Reformers defined salvation primarily in forensic terms, i.e., as justification, a declaration of pardon which is to be received by faith alone. They did not give serious enough attention to the truth that salvation also entails the healing of the brokenness and afflictions of man. Modern liberal theology has contributed to the loss of the healing ministry within Protestantism by explaining away the healing miracles of the New Testament as rational occurrences. A frequent interpretation of the healings given by liberal theologians is that they were the result of suggestion if not hypnotism.[1] The Bultmannian school understands the miracles as having been created by the later tradition of wonder stories out of what were originally symbolic acts.[2]

[1] See for example S. Vernon McCasland, *By the Finger of God* (N.Y.: Macmillan, 1951); and E. R. Micklem, *Miracles and the New Psychology* (London: Humphrey Milford, 1922).

[2] Reginald Fuller and Alan Richardson follow this general pattern of thought without denying, however, the historicity of many of the miracles. They both contend that the significance of the miracles is in their symbolism

It is becoming commonplace to speak of our age as one of anxiety. Mental illness has become a national malady. Suicide is on the uprise particularly among the young. Hundreds of thousands have become dependent upon tranquilizers in order to get through a day's work. Doctors are becoming increasingly aware of the interdependence of mind and body and consequently have begun pointing to the need for psychosomatic medicine. The ministry of healing has become indispensable for the church of our time.

There are signs that the churches or at least segments of the church are beginning to awaken to their responsibilities in this area. Among avant garde Roman Catholics extreme unction is being interpreted more as a sacrament of healing than as the last rites. Evangelical religious communities such as Iona, Bethany Fellowship and Lee Abbey are giving increasing attention to the healing ministry. New healing orders have arisen such as the Order of St. Luke the Physician, which has its roots mainly in the Episcopal church. The Mennonite church is pioneering in the area of mental health clinics.[3] The Seventh Day Adventists support over a hundred hospitals and have recently founded the pioneer Battle Creek sanitarium for the treatment of nervous disorders. Healing services are multiplying in such mainline churches as the Episcopal, Methodist and Presbyterian. A growing number of clergymen and laymen are embarked on special ministries of healing.[4]

Theologians also have begun to recognize the place of healing in the ministry of the church. Thurneysen includes healing within pastoral care, "the cure of souls," which is a necessary element in the ministry of every pastor. Barth maintains that healing is one of the essential ministries of the church.[5] Tillich has defined salvation mainly in terms of healing and thereby has prepared the way for dialogue between theology and psychotherapy.

In the scientific world the germ theory of disease is now under

of religious truths rather than in their actual occurrence. According to these men the miracles are acted out parables rather than signs of supernatural intervention. See Reginald Fuller, *Interpreting the Miracles* (Naperville: SCM, 1963); and Alan Richardson, *The Miracle-Stories of the Gospels* (N.Y.: Harper, n.d.).

[3] See the articles by Otto D. Klassen in *McCormick Quarterly*, Vol. XXI (July, 1967), pp. 23-54.

[4] On some of the new healing ministries see Emily Gardiner Neal, *God Can Heal You Now* (Englewood Cliffs, N.Y.: Prentice-Hall, 1964), pp. 135ff.

[5] Karl Barth, *Church Dogmatics*, IV, 3, b, trans. G. W. Bromiley (Edinburgh: T. & T. Clark, 1962), pp. 885-887.

heavy criticism. Germs to be sure are present in everyone, but
medical science is unable to explain what makes certain people
more susceptible to germs than others. Some doctors are ready
to acknowledge that sickness is fundamentally a spiritual problem rather than a physical one.[6] Behind physical and mental
affliction lies a broken relationship between man and his
neighbor and man and his God. This truth has been rediscovered
by such searching Christian laymen as Glenn Clark, Bernard
Martin, Emily Gardiner Neal, Agnes Sanford and many others.

## THEOLOGICAL BASIS FOR HEALING

It must be acknowledged that Christ is the healer as well
as the mediator and redeemer. Christ saves the whole man, and
this includes the healing of both his body and soul. As Paul
cogently expressed it: "If the Spirit of him who raised Jesus from
the dead dwells in you, he who raised Christ Jesus from the
dead will give life to your mortal bodies also through his Spirit
which dwells in you" (Rom. 8:11). Salvation entails the restoration of the body of man as well as the renewal of his spirit.

Salvation and health are closely related in the Bible.[7] The
Psalmist affirms: "Some were sick through their sinful ways,
and because of their iniquities suffered affliction. . . . Then they
cried to the Lord in their trouble, and he delivered them from
their distress; he sent forth his word and healed them" (Ps. 107:
17-20; cf. 41:3, 4; 103:3). Proverbs asserts that the fear of God
and turning from evil "will be healing to your flesh and
refreshment to your bones" (3:8; cf. 4:20-22). Jeremiah gives
this description of salvation: "For I will restore health to you,
and your wounds I will heal, says the Lord" (30:17; cf. 17:14).
The prophet Malachi foretells the rising of the sun of righteousness "with healing in its wings" (4:2).

In the New Testament the term salvation (soteria) and its
derivatives are even more closely related to bodily and emotional
health. This can especially be seen in Ac. 4:7-12 where the
healing of the cripple by Peter is regarded as tantamount to
salvation. That healing is an integral part of the Gospel ministry
can be seen in the commissioning of the disciples by Jesus: "And
he called the twelve together and gave them power and authority over all demons and to cure diseases, and he sent them out

---

[6] See S. I. McMillen, *None of These Diseases* (Westwood, New Jersey:
Revell, 1963).

[7] See Dorothee Hoch, *Healing and Salvation* (London: SCM, 1958), pp.
9-20.

to preach the kingdom of God and to heal" (Lk. 9:1, 2; cf. Mt. 10:8). Jesus believed His own mission to entail not only the preaching of the good news but also the liberating of the oppressed and the restoring of sight to the blind (Lk. 4:18).

The healing power of Christ, which is none other than the power of His cross and resurrection, is available for the whole world. Indeed, Christ died not only for the church but for humanity. Yet we are told that His salvation generally benefits only those who seek help from God or those who are objects of the concern of people who seek God's aid. The healing power of Christ must be appropriated in repentance and faith.

Scripture teaches that God heals by natural as well as supernatural means. This can be seen in II Kings where Hezekiah applies a cake of figs to the source of affliction (20:1-7). In Jn. 9:6, we read that Jesus made clay and anointed the eyes of the blind man and then told him to wash in the pool of Siloam. To be sure the miraculous character of the healings of Christ is more evident where there are no material means employed. But it is to be recognized that every genuine healing partakes of the miraculous. Yet we must also acknowledge that Christ is not limited to what is humanly possible or even conceivably possible in the kind of world in which we live. To affirm the healing ministry also means to affirm miracles in the narrow sense, i.e., divine intervention in the processes of nature.

Faith is seen in Scripture as the general precondition for healing. When Jesus was among His own people He could do no mighty work there because of their unbelief (Mk. 6:4-6). It is faith that restores men to health and salvation (cf. Mk. 10:52; Lk. 17:19; Mt. 9:22; Ac. 3:16). Faith is not only the condition but indeed the means of healing, and yet the glory belongs to God alone, since faith is a gift of God.

Prayer is also a means of healing. By prayer we understand not meditation as such but supplication and intercession. The apostle James reminds us that the prayer of faith will save the sick man (Jms. 5:15) and that by praying for one another we may be healed (5:16). Jesus asserts that there are some demons that can be cast out only by prayer and fasting (Mt. 17:21). Prayer indeed is the soul of faith (Calvin); it is faith in action and thereby a means to healing and salvation.

God to be sure does not always answer our prayers in the way we desire. We might be healed by prayer, but if we are not healed this does not necessarily mean that we lack faith. Job was torn by many afflictions, and yet he was a man of deep faith. It is well to bear in mind, however, that only after Job confessed his effrontery in seeking to justify God was he restored to health. We can pray for healing, but God may withhold this blessing from us until we pray in a contrite spirit. Or we may pray for bodily healing, and God will answer our prayer by healing our spirit. What is important to understand is that God wills full health and salvation for all of His children, but He will grant this gift in His own way and in His own time.

It can be said that God wills health especially for those who seek it in Christ and who seek it in accord with His will concerning their vocation. He permits sickness in order to test and discipline us and also to remind us that we are still living at least partly in the old aeon. The fact that the age to come is already here, however, means that power over sickness is available now.

We should pray for health not as an end in itself but as a means to deeper communion with God and greater freedom for service in His kingdom. Our goal should not be a long life on earth but a life that is pleasing to God, one that redounds to His glory. When we seek first His kingdom, other blessings will be given to us as well, very probably including health (Mt. 6:25-33). In his prayers for healing a dying person should surely pray primarily for deeper fellowship with Christ and consider the possibility that this might occur through death as well as through a physical healing.

The New Testament also speaks of a rite of healing and a charism of healing. The rite of healing entails the laying on of hands (cf. Ac. 28:8, 9) and sometimes an anointing with oil (Mk. 6:13; Jms. 5:14). The charism of healing (I Cor. 12:9) refers to a special gift which enables certain people to act and pray effectually for the healing of others. The power of healing is given to the whole church, and it is conveyed principally by intercessory prayer. All Christians, therefore, share in the ministry of healing, but only some are given the charismatic gift of healing and might therefore be commissioned as healers.

### THE PROBLEM OF SICKNESS

For too long Christians have been under the delusion that sickness is God's will for man. Biblical faith tells us that sickness is against the revealed will of God concerning His final purpose. Sickness belongs to the nothingness, the chaos which has been conquered by Christ. It should be placed in the same category as sin and death. At the same time sickness may be utilized by God in the plan of salvation. God might even sanction sickness as a means of strengthening faith or bringing men to faith. But God permits sickness to continue in the world only for a time — until the glory of His kingdom is made manifest. Because of the victory of Christ the children of God can even now be free from the curse of sickness, from its controlling power, although a vulnerability to sickness lingers on even among the saints because of the presence of sin.

This brings us to the relationship between sickness and sin. Whereas for the ancient Greeks moral disorder is rooted in physical disorder, the Hebrews held that the key to physical illness lies in the moral and spiritual realm. The Bible tells us that it is sin that makes sickness possible although no particular sickness is necessarily directly caused by sin. In the case of the paralytic who was healed by Jesus, sin was the immediate cause of his malady (Mk. 2:1-12; Lk. 5:17-26). But in the case of the man who was born blind (Jn. 9:1-3) we are told that neither he nor his parents had sinned. Rather his blindness was given to him so that the works of God might be made manifest in his life. Yet the fact that his healing was the first step in his salvation points to the truth that sickness belongs to the domain of sin. It might be said that sickness is a consequence of sin but not necessarily a punishment for sin.

It is well to note that Jesus who was sinless was never sick. To be sure he was susceptible to injury; indeed, he was crucified on a cross. But there is a palpable difference between external injury and internal disease, between a good apple that is knocked to the ground and an apple that simply rots away. The true man, the authentic man, cannot get sick because his life is centered in God, and this is the goal towards which all men of faith are directed.

The New Testament tells us that the ultimate source of sickness is the devil, the eternal adversary of God. It is the devil that causes pains and afflictions. Jesus saw His healings as victories over the demonic powers of darkness.[8] This does not mean that every healing is an exorcism, since the devil may cause sickness but not reign in the soul of the sick person. Most diseases and afflictions can be alleviated and counteracted by natural means, since these means are God-given. The cure will

---

[8] See James Kallas, *The Significance of the Synoptic Miracles* (Greenwich, Conn.: Seabury, 1961), pp. 38f.

not be complete, however, until man's spirit is brought into subjection to the Holy Spirit of God.

Karl Barth's significant contribution to the ministry of healing is that he has linked sickness with what God does not will rather than with what God wills, with the darkness that God rejects rather than with the light. Barth maintains that sickness is excluded from the new creation and that it continues to exist only by divine permission. Because sickness is never God's ultimate or final will, we must take care not to conclude our prayers for the sick with the words "if it be God's will."[9] We must pray with the confidence that all things work together for good for those who love God (Rom. 8:28). Nor should we affirm without reservation that one's sickness is for the glory of God. What is for the glory of God may happen in the sickness and in spite of it, but neither sickness nor sin of themselves glorify God.

## DEMON POSSESSION

Demon possession is the one malady that cannot be touched by natural means. Such possession might be defined as the total control of the will by an external, supernatural evil power, called in Christian tradition, the devil, Satan, the prince of the world, etc. To speak of "devils" is simply to refer to invisible agents and servants of the prince of darkness. There are no demons in the sense of disembodied spirits who incarnate themselves in persons. This is the primitive conception, and we shall presently seek to distinguish the view of biblical faith from that of primitive religion.

Demonology was one of the first casualties in the rising tide of post-Reformation liberal theology. The existence of demons was first generally doubted in the Enlightenment. Freud echoed the viewpoint of modern man when he declared in his *Totem and Taboo:* "It would be another matter if demons really existed. But we know that, like gods, they are creations of the human mind."[10] Vernon McCasland explains away demon possession with the tools of modern psychology.[11] He does not deny the historicity of the exorcisms but rather reinterprets them as psychological cures. Ernst Käsemann holds that demon pos-

---

9 It is proper to pray that God's will be done in the life of the afflicted person, but we should not suggest in our prayers that God's will is that this person remain in sickness.

10 James Strachey, ed. and trans., *The Complete Psychological Works of Sigmund Freud,* Vol. XIII (London: Hogarth Press, 1964), p. 24.

11 See S. Vernon McCasland, *By the Finger of God.*

session in the New Testament signifies that man is helpless to help himself. Tillich reinterprets the demons as transpersonal sociological powers which force men into bondage. The question is, however, whether impersonal forces can give concrete rational direction to man. Can there be temptation apart from a personal tempter? We can also ask those who psychologize the demons whether demonic temptation can arise out of the unconscious, since such temptations presuppose an overall strategy of evil. Among theologians in the modern age who have sought to retain the biblical perspective of demonology are Karl Heim, Louis Monden, Norval Geldenhuys, P. T. Forsyth, Gustaf Aulén, Gustaf Wingren, G. C. Berkouwer, Helmut Thielicke, and Eduard Thurneysen. Some psychiatrists and medical men including Theodore Bovet, A. Lechler, M. E. Obermayer, Thomas V. Moore, Bernard Martin, and Jean Lhermitte as well as pastoral psychologists like Kurt Koch and Charles Corcoran also affirm the existence of supernatural demonic powers.[12]

We concur fully in the judgment of Thurneysen:

> The demonological view of illness and sin in Holy Scripture is not to be regarded as surpassed by modern psychology and psychotherapy. Whatever psychopathic phenomena may come to light through psychological probing, they are not the primary cause according to biblical thought; they are the reflection and refraction of that metaphysical bondage to the powers of darkness to which sin has subjected man.[13]

Too often demon possession as a state of spiritual bondage is dismissed by modern thinkers because of its association with primitive mythological religion. Yet there is a marked difference between the primitive and biblical views on demonology.[14] We affirm this while at the same time recognizing the intrusion of primitive conceptions into the biblical story.[15] First of all in

---

12 See esp. Kurt Koch, *Seelsorge und Okkultismus* (Reith-Wusenteroth, 1953); and Jean Lhermitte, *True and False Possession*, trans. P. J. Hepburne-Scott (N.Y.: Hawthorne, 1963).

13 Eduard Thurneysen, *A Theology of Pastoral Care*, trans. Jack Worthington and Thomas Wieser (Richmond: John Knox, 1962), p. 325.

14 See Anton Fridrichsen, "The Conflict of Jesus With the Unclean Spirits" in *Theology*, Vol. XXII, No. 129 (March, 1931), pp. 122-135.

15 The exorcism of the Gerasene demoniac with demons entering the herd of swine (Mk. 5:1-20) should be understood as an attempt to interpret the victory over the demons in the language of the time. The swine were possibly driven into the sea by panic brought about by the sudden change in the possessed man. Again, they may have been driven into irrational fear by the ire of the demonic powers, or they may have sensed the presence of the diabolical. But we do not believe after the manner of primitive religion

biblical faith the demons are controlled and directed by One center of evil. In primitive religion each demon is a law unto itself and acts irrationally rather than according to a predetermined pattern and purpose. In biblical religion demon possession is always related to personal sin, whereas in primitive circles it is attributed to misfortune. Again, in the Bible the demons are fallen angels and therefore belong to a sphere higher than that of man. In primitive religion, demons are disembodied spirits, goblins, that come out of the nether world. In the biblical view, the devil is a superhuman anti-divine being whereas the demons of primitive mythology are subhuman earthbound spirits. This is to acknowledge the truth that the demonic powers like the angelic powers can only be described in the imaginative picture language of myth, but symbols always point to a literal reality. We affirm a literal devil, but we can describe this devil only in the language of symbolism.

It is likewise a mistake to confuse demon possession with psychosomatic illness although some illnesses that have been diagnosed as psychosomatic are in reality signs of possession. We recognize that what past ages often called demon possession would probably now prove to be forms of mental illness. There is a danger in drawing too close a connection between mental illness and demon possession. A "normal" person can also be demon possessed, and such persons may indeed be more bound to radical evil than a psychological misfit. Mental illness signifies a disorder of the mind whereas demon possession represents the bondage of the will to radical evil. At the same time one must not discount the fact that psychic illness may in some cases be a symptom and manifestation of spiritual slavery to evil powers.[16]

Demon possession may be indicated where men are moved by an overpowering compulsion either to self-destruction or to the destruction of others. It could be present in such afflictions as psychopathic criminality, chronic alcoholism, uncontrollable lust (especially perverse lust), inordinate hatred, and dope addiction. Yet we must utter here a word of caution. Such maladies do not necessarily signify demonic possession, but it is in these areas that the demons are especially active. The story has been

---

that either the demoniac or the swine were indwelt by bodiless ghoulish spirits.

16 According to the New Testament scholar Gerald Sloyan, the epileptic demoniac in Mk. 9:14-24 is the case of an epileptic who was really possessed by a demon. His seizure was very unlike that of most epileptics. See Gerald S. Sloyan, *The Gospel of St. Mark* (Collegeville, Minn.: Liturgical Press, 1960), pp. 85-87.

told to this author of a prominent New York pastor who was ministering to a woman dope addict who had made several attempts at suicide. She had been in and out of sanitariums and prisons and had been pronounced incurable. Finally one evening after the addict had given up all hope, the pastor, a liberal in his theological orientation but also desperate for a remedy, addressed himself to the demon and ordered this spirit in the name of Jesus Christ to release his hold upon his victim. The demonic spirit obeyed, though only after the woman had experienced much inner agony and tribulation. But the outcome was that the woman was freed, and she has never relapsed since that incident. Even in this age of science and in a nation where psychology is king, there is still a place for demon exorcism.

One must be careful again to differentiate demon exorcism as biblical theology understands it and the primitive conception of exorcism. The names of the demons should be understood as representing desires implanted in the heart by Satan, e.g., death, lust and hatred. The voices of the demons, which are regarded as so significant in primitive religious circles, should generally be interpreted as the voices of the other self, the alter-ego, although the content of what is said may very well be directed by the devil. At the same time a "split personality" or "multiple personality" does not always connote possession; it could signify incomplete possession, since there are still aspects of the personality not under the control of Satan. Medical and spiritual diagnoses frequently overlap, but here again we must caution against drawing too close a correlation between psychic abnormality and a state of possession.

In our view being a prisoner of Satan is not simply another name for being a servant of sin. All servants of sin are in one sense servants of Satan in that sin is the will of the devil and not the will of God. Yet to be a prisoner of Satan in the full sense means that one must choose just as the devil chooses. Sinners as such still have the freedom to choose between greater and lesser evils. Theodore Hegre is helpful here in his distinction between oppression by the devil and possession by the devil.[17] All people, including Christians, are oppressed by the devil, but only a few become wholly possessed.[18]

---

[17] Theodore Hegre, *"The Will of God Your Sanctification"* (Minneapolis: Bethany Fellowship, 1961), pp. 83-87.

[18] In contrast to some of the sects we hold that those who believe in Christ can never be possessed by the demonic, since the devil is powerless where Christ is present.

The power of the devil can especially be seen where crowds and nations become possessed. Demons are particularly virulent when they become incarnate in social institutions. This means that the institution is no longer in the hands of men but is in the grip of forces beyond the control of man. Nor are these forces merely impersonal as Tillich would have us believe; they reflect an overarching strategy and purpose. The mass insanity that afflicted Germany under Hitler was described by some observers as a demonic spell. This is a more profound diagnosis of the situation than that advanced by social psychologists who attributed the blind fanaticism of the Nazis to emotional hysteria.

Jesus Christ mortally wounded the principalities and powers by His death and resurrection, but these powers are not yet destroyed. The grace of Christ is available for us now to overcome all sickness and sin. Christ is able to keep us from falling, but we are still susceptible to demonic temptation, and this means that the Christian life is a constant struggle against sin, death and the devil.

We are freed from demon possession not by incantations and magic but by the proclamation of the Gospel and the prayers of the church. There may be a place for a liturgy of exorcism in our churches. Exorcism simply means that the evil power is persuaded to relinquish his hold upon the afflicted. It does not mean that a disembodied spirit is literally cast out of the afflicted. The controlling power of evil is not inside of man but rather outside of man. The church must beware of pseudo-exorcism which is magic. Our reliance must not be on psychic dynamics and drama but on the word of the cross which alone is able to expel the demons. We should also recognize a charism of exorcism, which means that certain people are specially gifted at dealing with the curse of demon possession.

### DIVINE VS. MAGICAL HEALING

When Peter and John healed the man who had been lame from birth, Peter declared: "Men of Israel, why do you wonder at this, or why do you stare at us, as though by our own power or piety we had made him walk?" (Ac. 3:12). The apostle was pointing to an important truth that it is not the Christian who heals but rather Jesus Christ Himself. The Christian is only an instrument of the One who alone restores men to full health and salvation. Whenever men seek to arrogate to themselves the power of healing, then we are in the sphere of magic.

The fount of healing is not the powers of man but the cross of Christ (cf. I Pet. 2:24).

Magical healing might be defined as that which is effected by human technique and power, even mental power. One's dependence is no longer on God but upon certain formulas or rituals which are believed to have an automatic effect. Even medical healing can become partly magical if the doctor places his faith exclusively in his own techniques and powers and ignores the power of God.[19] The widespread uncritical reliance upon pills in modern society can surely be said to border upon magic. Magical healing is very much present in the cults such as New Thought and Christian Science which seek to effect cures by the repetition of certain affirmations and negations. It is also present in Catholic healing shrines where many people seek to be restored to health by making contact with miraculous medals and amulets, holy water and relics.[20] This is no longer divine healing but superstition. Pentecostalism is also not immune from magical healing particularly when the healing power is likened to an electric current (analogous to mana in primitive religion) which can be controlled and manipulated by the healer. Oral Roberts has often been accused of magical practices, but he has sought to overcome the theological deficiencies of his earlier days by attributing the healings solely to Christ. He has declared: "We preach, we lay hands on and we pray, but we can't heal or save anyone. We know that only Jesus can save and heal."[21] While continuing to have certain reservations concerning Oral Roberts' theology, we nevertheless believe that he has been given an authentic charism of healing and that his

---

[19] The presence of magic is even more evident in psychiatry and psychoanalysis which are not as controlled by scientific procedure as physical medicine. Dr. J. J. Eysenck, Professor of Psychology at London University, argues that the number of cures effected by psychoanalysis is no greater than that effected by hypnosis, the laying on of hands, dummy pills and suggestion. See Leslie Lieber, "Farewell to Freud," in *This Week Magazine, Des Moines Sunday Register* (Sept. 18, 1966), p. 5. Sebastian de Grazia contends that modern psychotherapy, particularly psychoanalysis, has much in common with the magical healing of primitive religion. See his *Errors of Psychotherapy* (Garden City, N.Y.: Doubleday, 1952).

[20] This is not to discount the many authentic healing miracles that have occurred at such shrines as Lourdes. Moreover, many of these cures have been subjected to intense medical scrutiny and have been found to be inexplicable on the basis of the canons of medical science. See Louis Monden, *Signs and Wonders* (N.Y.: Desclee, 1966), pp. 184f.; and Alexis Carrel, *The Voyage to Lourdes,* trans. Virgilia Peterson (N.Y.: Harper, 1950).

[21] *Abundant Life* (Nov., 1966), Vol. XX, No. 11, p. 23.

ministry has been instrumental in the healings of thousands who could not be helped by medical science.

As regards the cults that comprise the so-called metaphysical movement, New Thought, Christian Science and Unity, we hold that there is much truth in what they teach but that this truth is not seen in its proper context. We acknowledge that God may work through mental concentration or mental prayer. Paul urges us to fix our thoughts on those things that are edifying and uplifting (Phil. 4:8; Col. 3:2), and such thinking may be a means by which men are restored to wholeness and integrity. Yet we refuse to believe that there are spiritual laws which can be discovered and then applied. This would bind the grace of God to what is empirically demonstrable and verifiable. We acknowledge that there is such a thing as mental healing, i.e., healing engendered solely by the power of the mind, but this must not be confused with divine healing. Right thinking can cure many ailments, but only the grace of God can heal all ailments. Mental healing in the technical sense still lies in the sphere of the psychological whereas divine healing breaks into the psychological from the beyond. There is a marked difference between what the neo-transcendentalists call metaphysical healing and what might be termed messianic healing, i.e., healing that springs from faith in a personal messiah. As we have said God may be present in our thinking and meditation. Edifying ideas may be vehicles through which God's grace is conveyed. Yet we must also bear in mind that God "is able to do far more abundantly than all that we ask or think" (Eph. 3:20).

There is a place for healing aids, rituals and liturgies in the ministry of healing. Yet one must be careful never to attribute a healing or redemptive power to the rituals and aids, for this borders upon magic. Indeed, we must beware of attributing a redemptive power even to our faith understood as our own work or obedience. In the deepest sense "faith healing" is not yet divine healing. It is not the psychic act of believing but the grace of God that restores man to health. A Christian psychiatrist gives this warning against magical healing:

> When "magic" is mixed up in it, there is no real healing. There is nearly always the transposition of evil from one area to another. What is the good of healing the body, if the mind becomes sick? What is the good of healing the mind, if that involves the loss of the soul?[22]

22 Bernard Martin, *Healing for You*, trans. A. A. Jones (Richmond: John Knox, 1965).

Just as God may work through mental prayer so He also may and does work through psychiatry and medicine. Those churches that are fascinated with divine healing must not neglect the contributions of scientific healing. As Sirach enjoined: ". . . give the physician his place, for the Lord created him, let him not leave you, for there is need of him" (Sirach 38:12). There is a place for church hospitals, medical missions, and church mental health clinics. But the Christian doctor unlike his secular counterpart will recognize that full healing involves the spirit of man, the inner man. The most that medical science can do is to repair damaged ligaments and organs. It can restore men to a proper working condition, but it cannot give them a new horizon, a purpose and direction, a new life, which the grace of God alone can provide. This is why medical care needs to be grounded in and supplemented by prayer and faith if it is to effect the healing of the whole man. It is interesting to note that at the Chikore Hospital in rural Rhodesia the hospital staff have recognized the spiritual dimension of the illnesses of their African patients by undergirding medical treatment with spiritual counsel.[23]

In our view the healing power of God is given through prayer and faith primarily and through medicine and psychiatry secondarily. Medicine is a material cause but not an efficient cause in authentic healing. This is why the early Christians first called upon the elders when they became sick rather than the doctors (Jms. 5:14; cf. II Chron. 16:12).

All Christians share in the healing ministry. But as some have been given special gifts, there is consequently a place for an ordination to the healing ministry. It may also be proper on occasion to hold healing services in the local church, but such services should not become the focal point of the church's ministry. The principal source of healing is none other than the proclamation of the Word, and if the Word is being rightly proclaimed it should contribute to the healing of men as well as to their justification. There may be a place, as has been said, for healing rites such as that practiced in the Church of the Brethren (consisting in an anointing with oil and laying on of hands). Prayer groups in a church devoted to intercession can also be a potent arm of the healing ministry of the church.

What is most important to realize is that Christ the living Lord has come to save us from sickness as well as sin and death.

---

[23] J. Franklin Donaldson, "Do Witch Doctors Have Something?" in *United Church Herald* (May, 1968), Vol. II, No. 5, pp. 18-25.

He has come not only to forgive all our iniquity but also to heal all our diseases (Ps. 103:3). He will not pardon us and yet leave us in our afflictions. Salvation entails not only the remission of sins but also the healing of mind, soul and body. Although the death of the body is the inevitable consequence of sin, we can be assured that we shall inherit an incorruptible, eternal body which is already taking form in our present existence. Man's final destiny is perfect wholeness and well-being. Full salvation indeed entails perfect health.

One should be wary of seeking special gifts such as healing and exorcism without at the same time seeking the Divine Healer, Jesus Christ. Our attention should be focused not so much upon the gifts as upon the Giver. He will make known to us if it is His will that we exercise such gifts. If we open ourselves to His Spirit, we shall then be inwardly filled, and this may entail our own healing as well as the receiving of gifts and talents that can enable us to help others. It is possible to be healed of a specific disease and even to have a special charism of healing and still be without the Savior, Jesus Christ. If our healing is to be complete it must entail repentance and faith, since full healing in the Christian sense signifies the restoration of an estranged relationship with God.

The healing ministry should serve the ministry of the Word, since divine healing is a sign and witness of the salvation of Christ. The primary mission of the church is the preaching of the Gospel and the saving of souls, but healing can be both a fruit of this salvation and a stepping-stone to it. Such healers as Kathryn Kulman see evangelism as their principal calling, but healing plays an integral role in this calling. The final goal of the ministry of healing should be the conversion of men and women to Jesus Christ. This is why such a ministry will give primary attention to spiritual healing, the healing of the inward man. Indeed, the key to total recovery from any illness or malady is spiritual regeneration.

ELEVEN:

# EVANGELISM IN A SECULAR AGE

## THE PRESENT STATUS OF EVANGELISM

Evangelism is once again under discussion at theological meetings and church conferences. As the nation and the world become steadily more secularized, the need to communicate the Gospel becomes all the more acute. New missionary strategies are being employed in order to reach the emerging pagan masses with the message of Christ.

Among the types of evangelism currently in vogue is visitation evangelism. Its aim is generally church affiliation rather than conversion to Christ. At its best it can become a means whereby people are led either directly or indirectly into confrontation with the Christian message. The Jehovah's Witnesses and Mormons have demonstrated that house-to-house visitation can win over many who were previously undecided or even hostile to religion. At its worst this kind of evangelism can degenerate into a form of proselytism which is little more than a blatant bid for recruits. The concern is no longer to introduce men and women to Jesus Christ but rather to build up the institution. Instead of reaching the lost the visitation evangelist frequently steals sheep from other folds.

One modern prophet makes this criticism:

> Again, one wonders about the usefulness of visitation evangelism when the literature seems to assume that this great emphasis in many of our denominations is designed primarily to locate the people in the community, who, by their background and culture, are logically part of a fellowship of our church. It may legitimately fit under the heading of evangelism, but too often this method nets only men and women who have already been within the orbit of Christian faith. One doubts its effectiveness in confronting the pagans who are emerging in our midst in modern life. In a word it does not presuppose a radical missionary situation but is rather a form of recruitment for our churches.[1]

[1] George W. Webber, *God's Colony In Man's World* (Nashville: Abingdon, 1960), p. 38.

One successful venture in visitation evangelism is that under-taken by the Coral Ridge Presbyterian Church in Fort Lauder-dale, Florida, under the pastoral leadership of D. James Kennedy. The church sponsors a clinic on evangelism which is held once a year. The mornings are devoted to intensive training sessions on prayer, lectures, mock situations and question and answer sessions. In the evenings each participant in the clinic accompanies one of the trained personnel on visits in the community where he receives "on-the-job" training. The purpose of this kind of evangelism is not simply to invite people into the fellowship of the church but to confront them with the truth of the Christian Gospel. The visitation evangelists are trained to witness to the Gospel and lead men to Christ. When the call to decision is given in the church the following Sunday many of those who respond are reaffirming the decision that they already made in their homes during the week. The church has grown phenomenally in membership in the past few years — from less than one hundred to more than a thousand. One danger in the approach at Coral Ridge is that the Gospel may sometimes be treated as a product that can be sold and delivered. But the Gospel is not something we possess but rather that which possesses us. We can tell people about the Gospel and point them to it, but we cannot hand it over to them. Evan-gelism is not salesmanship by which we seek to dispense our wares but rather sharing the faith in love.

The experiment at Coral Ridge reflects the impact of revival-ism upon the American religious scene. There is currently much discussion concerning the role of revival meetings and crusades in the missionary strategy of the church today. Particularly we need to examine mass evangelism as exemplified by the Billy Graham crusades.

The hallmark of modern-day revivalism is "the altar call" by which sinners are directed to come forward to the front of the sanctuary where they can make a public decision for Christ. This was a technique first adopted by the evangelist Charles Finney. The place where the penitents were congregated was originally known as "the anxious seat" and "the mourners' bench." Dwight L. Moody introduced inquiry rooms which pro-vide those who seek conversion some degree of privacy. This method is also followed today by Billy Graham. The altar call gives people a concrete opportunity for decision and rededica-tion. The revivals that have been conducted by Moody and today by Billy Graham and Bryan Green have proved a blessing to countless thousands who otherwise might never have been moved to commit their lives to Jesus Christ.

Modern mass evangelism is not, however, without its dangers. In many of the mass revival meetings it is possible to discern a subtle accommodation to the values of the business culture. There is an emphasis on numbers and bigness which reflects the spirit of American capitalism. Moody had resisted the temptation to keep numbers, but since the evangelist Gipsy Smith the number of decisions has been carefully tabulated and advertised. The reliance upon the findings of psychology particularly in the advertising of the evangelistic campaign betrays a desire to manipulate rather than to proclaim. Conversion to Christ is sometimes understood as a purely human act of the will which can be induced by psychological means. Charles Finney said that conversion to saving faith "is not a miracle, or dependent on a miracle in any sense" but "is a purely philosophical result of the right use of the constitutional means."[2] Such a view signifies a marked deviation from the principles of the evangelical theology of the Reformation. It also contrasts with the views of Jonathan Edwards who spoke of the revival as "the surprising work of God."

The peril of synergistic theology also makes its appearance in much of modern revivalism. We are sometimes told to give our hearts to Christ, and then regeneration will be effected by the Spirit. But this betrays a Pelagian theology, for one cannot confess his sins and surrender to Christ unless regeneration by the Spirit is already taking place. The man in sin cannot make a proper response to the Gospel message unless he has already received the Spirit. Graham's Calvinism generally prevents him from falling into synergism, but many lesser known evangelists are almost wholly Pelagian in their outlook. A hard-shell Calvinism is of course also deficient because it does not always consider the truth that conversion entails a response by man to the offer of God's grace as well as the work of the Spirit within man.

The evangelistic crusade can also become a means of cheap grace whereby the delusion is fostered that total regeneration is accomplished in a single moment of decision. In the older revivalism conversion was accompanied by much weeping and inward wrestling. But in what some sociological critics call "commercialized revivalism" becoming a Christian is sometimes pictured as almost too easy. One needs only to come to the altar

---

[2] Quoted in William G. McLoughlin, Jr., *Modern Revivalism: Charles Grandison Finney to Billy Graham* (N.Y.: Ronald, 1959), p. 11.

or simply to raise one's hand. It is true that the miracle of regeneration in its first stage is instantaneous, but it should be remembered that such a miracle does not take place apart from inward struggling and a profound conviction of sin. The early revivalists on the American frontier had gone with the people to their homes after the meetings and prayed and agonized with them.[3] But in later urban revivalism commitment was often reduced to a formal act of assent. The decision for Christ that one makes at a public meeting should not in all cases be equated with the new birth which the Holy Spirit brings about and which occurs only in conjunction with heartfelt repentance for sin. It is significant that the Billy Graham team now refers to the public decisions as inquiries rather than conversions.

We must also be on guard against the view rampant in the circles of modern revivalism that one can have complete assurance of his salvation if he has undergone a crisis experience of conversion. Assurance is indeed given to us in faith, but its locus is not our religious experience but rather the promises of God in Scripture. We can be certain of God's love, but we can never be certain enough of our own constancy and fidelity. The great evangelical theologian Jonathan Edwards held that assurance is something that has to be continually maintained in daily obedience. He declared: "All those who are converted are not sure of it; and those who are sure, do not know that they shall always be so; and still seeking and serving God with the utmost diligence, is the way to have assurance, and to have it maintained."[4]

Finally we must point to a lack of the prophetic dimension in much latter-day revivalism. Many revivalistic preachers are guilty of the sin of abstractionism, which means that they overlook the concrete sins which corrupt people and nations. They may very well inveigh against personal sins which are often infractions of cultural mores, but they leave untouched the social sins which poison the society in which men live. They will uphold Christ as the answer but will not show how He is the answer in the complex social situation in which men find themselves. The older liberal theology also succumbed to a kind of abstractionism when it upheld Love as the answer without

3 Bernard A. Weisberger, *They Gathered at the River* (Boston: Little, Brown, 1958), p. 206.

4 Jonathan Edwards, "Sermon: 'The Christian Pilgrim'" in *Works of President Edwards*, ed. Sereno E. Dwight, VII (N.Y.: S. Converse, 1829-1830), pp. 143-144.

giving concrete guidance to men concerning the critical issues of the time. In the evangelistic campaigns of Alan Walker in South Africa several years ago, the prophetic note was much more prominent, for he unabashedly condemned apartheid as a sin against God.[5] Billy Graham has also moved in the direction of deeper social concern and has publicly censured racial discrimination in all of its insidious forms. It is to be regretted that he has not raised his voice to the same degree against nationalism and militarism, but he has made clear that evangelistic preaching must be prophetic as well if it is to be relevant to our time and faithful to the Scriptures.

It should be recognized that evangelical revivalism in its earlier history was instrumental in bringing about much needed social reforms. We think here of William Wilberforce and the Clapham movement in the eighteenth century in England which helped rid that nation of slavery. John Wesley warned against slavery, drunkenness, political corruption and poverty. He himself established knitting guilds to enable poor women to make a living. Halle Pietism played an important role in the abolishing of drinking and dueling fraternities. The Finney revivals in America certainly contributed in no small measure to the abolition of slavery, prison reform and temperance. Charles Péan, the French Salvation Army evangelist, was partly responsible for the closing of the notorious French prison on Devil's Island. William Henry Harris in nineteenth-century England and the Blumhardts in Germany were all noted for their radical protests against social wrongs as well as their evangelical fervor. In recent years in America prohibition has been the only real social issue which concerned the revivalists. In some revival circles today the welfare state and Communism are considered the principal social evils. This is not presently true of the Billy Graham team, but it does hold true for many lesser known revivalists who seem often to be allied with right-wing extremism.

In our view evangelical revivalism still has much to contribute to the advancement of the kingdom in our day. The mass evangelistic crusades reach hundreds of thousands who would otherwise remain lost in their sins. Billy Graham and a few of the other notable evangelists of our time have shown themselves to be cognizant of the dangers in this approach, and they themselves remind us that mass evangelism cannot stand by itself but

---

[5] See Harold Henderson, "Alan Walker in South Africa" in *The Christian Century*, Vol. LXXX, No. 46 (Nov. 13, 1963), pp. 1410-1412.

must be united with other kinds of missionary strategy. Graham acknowledges that one reason why so many converts fall away after the initial experience is that they are not nurtured in churches that are centered in the Gospel. We need also to be particularly alert to the dangers of a dependence upon psychological techniques rather than the power of the Holy Spirit in an evangelistic campaign. We should give serious consideration to these questions of Dr. Martin Lloyd-Jones, former pastor of Westminster Chapel, London:

> Are we to be primarily and almost exclusively concerned with evangelistic campaigns and with the attempt to make them more efficient by new methods and techniques? Or, should we not concentrate more, as the Church has done throughout the centuries, upon praying for, and laying the basis of Christian instruction for, revival as it is described in the Bible? Should we not pray with greater earnestness for a visitation of God's Holy Spirit both upon the Church and upon ourselves as individuals?[6]

Our position is that an evangelistic crusade can prepare the way for a genuine spiritual revival. But Dr. Martin Lloyd-Jones and others rightly remind us that such a crusade must not be confused with the spiritual revival itself, which is essentially a work of the Holy Spirit. Our age has yet to experience the widespread moving of the Spirit over our churches and our nation, and this means that despite our campaigns and crusades spiritual renewal or revival is still a goal rather than a fact.

Dietrich Bonhoeffer has wisely observed that the American church has had many revivals but not a genuine reformation.[7] Revival usually connotes the restoration of older forms of devotion and piety. Reformation means bringing the piety, the organization, and doctrines of the church under the criticism of the Word of God. It signifies not only changing the lives of individual Christians but changing the church itself. There is no question that the church itself needs to be drastically reformed in our time. And yet we must not lose sight of the complementary truth that genuine reformation cannot succeed unless men and women are personally converted from the way of sin to the way of righteousness. We need both revival and reformation, but the revival will not be complete unless a reforma-

---

6 Martin Lloyd-Jones, *Conversions Psychological and Spiritual* (London: Inter-Varsity Fellowship, 1965), p. 40.

7 Dietrich Bonhoeffer, *No Rusty Swords*, trans. Edwin H. Robertson and John Bowden (N.Y.: Harper & Row, 1965), p. 117.

tion also takes place that will affect not only the church but the society in which we live.

## THE NEW EVANGELISM

A new kind of evangelism has appeared in our time which signifies a marked reaction against the religious imperialism, individualism and perfectionism that have frequently marred the evangelical movement and the institutional church. This evangelism often goes under the name of secular evangelism and sometimes ecumenical evangelism. It is none other than the missionary strategy proposed by secular theology and secular ecumenism. According to this kind of theology the evangelistic task is not simply to bring about commitment to Christ but rather commitment through Christ to ministry in the world. The goal of evangelism is the service of our neighbor and not primarily the saving of souls. Theologians associated with the new theology and ipso facto with the new evangelism are John Robinson, Harvey Cox, Gibson Winter, Jitsuo Morikawa, Colin Williams, and Malcolm Boyd. All of these men stress the need to witness by life and example. Their emphasis is not so much upon the Christian proclamation as upon a Christian style of life. The term "Christian presence" is often used in the circles of the new evangelism. This simply means being with and for people in their tribulation and dereliction. It is to be contrasted with preaching at people. Religious communities in Protestantism and Roman Catholicism that partly or wholly subscribe to this new evangelistic strategy are Iona, Taizé, Imshausen in Germany, and the Community for Christian Service.

One of the principal emphases of the new evangelism is the reform of society. According to Bishop Robinson evangelism consists not so much in converting as in the socializing and humanizing of broken, alienated men. Jitsuo Morikawa, secretary of evangelism of the American Baptist convention, has declared: "Contemporary evangelism is moving away from winning souls one by one, to the evangelization of the structures of the society."[8] Social action therefore becomes the pivotal element in evangelism. Harvey Cox contends that "evangelism, the speaking about God is political. . . . Standing in a picket line is a way of speaking. By doing it a Christian speaks of God."[9] George Web-

---

[8] Quoted in *Christianity Today*, Vol. 8, No. 12 (March 13, 1964), p. 26.
[9] Harvey Cox, *The Secular City* (N.Y.: Macmillan, 1965), p. 256.

ber has made this astounding statement: "In short, evangelism, in its varied dimensions, is politics."[10]

Service to the world is the key note of the new evangelism. Some of the representatives of this movement speak of an evangelism of identification, which they contrast with an evangelism of decision. Solidarity with the world, not separation from the world, should be the missionary strategy of the church in our time. Robert Raines argues that relevant witness takes place where Christians become servants to those in the world who stand in need. It is not a "telling witness" so much as an "answering witness."[11] This is to say, it is a witness in terms of our response to a world made curious by the shape of our service. Ronan Hoffman, a Catholic expert on missiology, also shares this general view; at a missionary conference in Washington, D.C., in September of 1967 he urged his brethren to dismantle the missions structure and start "humanizing" mankind through secular evolution.[12]

Another hallmark of the new evangelism is the emphasis upon dialogue as a means of witnessing. Robinson envisages his missionary theology as a venture in evangelism, as "a dialogue between religious man and secular man. And secular man is just as much inside the church as out of it, and just as much inside myself."[13] Gibson Winter speaks of a new mode of proclamation oriented about the needs of men, their problems and yearnings. He sees the point of contact with the secular man as the common struggle towards a new humanity. According to this approach communication entails listening to and then attempting to answer the existential questions of the culture. It involves discovering and wrestling with the problems of men. Here one can discern the influence of Tillich who believed that the church should begin not with divine revelation but with the questions of the culture. The Evangelical academies in Germany and the coffee house ministries generally mirror this kind of evangelism. It is well to note a recent Brother Juniper cartoon in which Juniper comes out of a coffee house saying, "The doughnuts were good, the coffee was strong but the theology was weak." What is so often given in the coffee house is not a definite

---

10 George W. Webber, *The Congregation in Mission* (Nashville: Abingdon, 1964), p. 67.

11 Robert Raines, *Reshaping the Christian Life* (N.Y.: Harper & Row, 1964), p. 68.

12 See *Christianity Today*, Vol. XII, No. 1 (Oct. 13, 1967), p. 43.

13 John Robinson, *The Honest to God Debate*, ed. David Edwards (Philadelphia: Westminster, 1963), p. 275.

message concerning absolute truth but rather a sympathetic ear
to the problems of the customers. Dialogic evangelism is founded
on the Socratic principle that truth is latent within man and
needs only to be drawn out. Reformation theology on the other
hand is based on the biblical view that the truth is not in man
and must therefore be announced to him by an outside authority.

We concur in the judgment of *Christianity Today* that the
the new evangelism seems to be a form of post-millennialism
looking to the establishment of the "city of man" on earth.[14]
Colin Williams has declared: "God is working in history toward
the goal of an open city in which the old middle walls are
dismantled. . . . We are to see these events . . . as God's call to join
him in the task of translating the final goals into the structures
of contemporary society."[15] Harvey Cox sees the dawning of
the kingdom of God in the secular city, and Gibson Winter
views the emerging metropolis as the new creation. In the new
theology the locus of God's revelation is events of social change
(Cox) or the freedom movement (Williams). The emphasis
is upon God speaking to us not in the Bible but in the world.
The means of salvation is no longer the good news but good
works. The arena of redemption is considered to be the present
struggle for social and racial equality. Reconciliation is viewed
in terms of the breaking down of the walls that divide the races
and classes in society rather than an act of God accomplished
in the death of Jesus Christ on the cross. Salvation is equated
with humanization and rehabilitation as sociologists understand
these terms rather than with justification and sanctification.

The question can be raised as to whether the new evangelism
is a new style apologetics. Some of the radical theologians such
as William Hamilton and Howard Moody seek to move beyond
apologetics to a silent ministry of suffering love. These men
appeal to Dietrich Bonhoeffer who boldly criticized apologetics
as a betrayal of the Gospel and who stressed witnessing by a life
of sacrificial service. Bonhoeffer, however, did not separate such
a witness from the evangelical proclamation, although he is
sometimes interpreted in this way. Most of the radical or secular theologians tend to follow the pattern set by Paul Tillich
who seeks to correlate the questions and strivings of the culture
and the Christian answer. The new evangelists for the most part
aim to convince the secular man both by word and deed of the
secular relevance of the faith. They seek to utilize the language

14 See *Christianity Today*, Vol. XI, No. 3 (Nov. 11, 1966), p. 32.
15 *Ibid.*

and categories of the secular world in order to reach the secular man for the Gospel. It is highly questionable, however, whether they are successful in actually bringing sinners into a saving relationship with Jesus Christ.

Another theologian who seems to be a major influence on the new evangelism and the new theology is Ernst Troeltsch. Like Hegel he conceived of an immanent world spirit realizing itself in the various religions and cultures of history. Troeltsch held that all religion is relative and that every culture generates its own type of religion; therefore it is a mistake to try to impose Western religious standards upon the East.[16] He believed in dialogue with non-Christian religions rather than missions. He still perceived the necessity for missionary work among primitive peoples, but our primary aim should be to uplift them by education. It is interesting to note that many of our larger denominations speak not of sending foreign missionaries abroad but rather fraternal workers who seek to share technical skills rather than preach a living Gospel.

John Dewey has also exerted a significant influence on the new evangelism in that his emphasis was on learning by doing. One no longer preaches an authoritative message but rather helps men to learn of the values of the Christian religion by enlisting them in a service project. In criticizing the Deweyite philosophy we must beware of relapsing into the notion popular in fundamentalist circles of learning by repetition. We fully agree with the view expressed in *Eternity* magazine:

> If the new evangelism has taken over Dewey's educational philosophy, perhaps the old evangelism may still be using a nineteenth century concept, 'learn by repetition.' Vain repetition of soul-winning phrases and meaningless procedures is no more to be valued than vain repetition in prayer.[17]

One of the chief fallacies of the new evangelism is the belief that salvation can be attained apart from conscious personal faith in the living Christ. All men are glibly spoken of as children of God and brothers in Christ without any study of the Scriptural meaning of these phrases. "Wherever there is love, there is Christ" might be regarded as a key slogan of the new evangelism. But we tend to forget that the love of Christ cannot be separated from His holiness and that one cannot there-

---

16 See Ernst Troeltsch, "The Place of Christianity Among the World Religions" in his *Christian Thought: Its History and Application* (N.Y.: Meridian Books, 1957), pp. 34-63.

17 *Eternity*, Vol. 18, No. 6 (June, 1967), p. 9.

fore know this love without being convicted of sin and driven to repentance. Tillich's view that all those who are not in the manifest (or visible) church are in the latent church is widely accepted by the secular and radical theologians. Niebuhr speaks of a hidden Christ who is everywhere present but particularly among the Jewish people who represent the old covenant; he has consequently declared himself opposed to missions to the Jews. Karl Rahner's concept of the "anonymous Christian," one who does the will of Christ without conscious faith in Him, also meets with approval in the circles of the new theology. When Hans Küng refers to the non-Christian religions as the ordinary way to salvation and the Christian faith as the extraordinary way, it would seem that he has taken the nerve out of missions.[18] D. T. Niles, who still has one foot in Christian orthodoxy, nevertheless declares that before the missionary arrives in a pagan country, Christ is already there. We hold that there can be no dynamic biblical evangelism unless salvation is correlated with faith, unless faith is seen to be the indispensable means of receiving the saving power and wisdom of God.

## TOWARDS A RESTATEMENT OF EVANGELISM

In order to reinterpret evangelism in the light of the New Testament we must associate it again with the *evangelion,* the good news concerning God's love revealed in Jesus Christ. Evangelism is the confronting of men with the evangelical kerygmatic proclamation and the call to repentance. It is essentially a verbal proclamation, since the biblical word is the means by which faith comes to us, and yet it must always be accompanied by deeds of loving concern. Its purpose should be seen as the conversion and re-dedication of sinful men. Evangelism is radically personal, since it has to do with the salvation of the lost sinner. But it also has a corporate dimension in that men should be called to repent of social as well as individual sins. Moreover, it entails an invitation to enter into the fellowship of the church where faith can be nurtured and deepened.

It can be seen that we conceive of evangelism as primarily the preaching of Jesus Christ and Him crucified. It surely should not be regarded as the prophetic involvement of Christians in society (as secular theologians maintain) nor simply as the worshiping, baptizing and educating of Christians (the general view in Eastern Orthodoxy). But we also maintain against Barth

18 See Hans Küng, *Freedom Today,* trans. Cecily Hastings (N.Y.: Sheed & Ward, 1965), pp. 109-161.

that in addressing ourselves to the world outside the church, we need to proclaim the law as well as the Gospel, the judgment as well as the love of God. Indeed, effective evangelism is the heralding of the whole Gospel, and this includes both the wrath and judgment of God against sin and the mercy of God revealed in the cross of Christ.

Moreover, we hold that all preaching should be partly evangelistic or kerygmatic. Christians too need to be converted, that is to say, their conversion needs to be deepened, since they continue to be afflicted by sin. Their regeneration has decisively begun, but it is not yet consummated. They are no longer under the controlling power of sin, but they are by no means free from the presence of sin. The condition of the Christian is, in the words of one of the old Gospel songs, "only a sinner saved by grace." And his salvation and conversion need to continue, since they are not complete. As Jonathan Edwards put it, "Our act of closing with and accepting Christ, is not in all respects completed by our accepting him with our hearts, 'til we have done it practically too, so have accepted him with the whole man, soul, spirit, and body."[19] In later evangelical revivalism the view was set forth that the sinner is instantaneously transformed in a crisis experience of conversion. We believe that one's incorporation into Christ is effected in a moment, but we are surely not transformed in a moment. So long as sin remains in us, we need to receive the medicine of the Word and sacrament, and this means that our conversion is a lifelong struggle. What is decisive for our salvation is not simply the initial step of faith but rather perseverance in conversion. Did not Jesus point out in the parable of the sower that only those who hear the Word of God and keep it are truly elected for the kingdom (Lk. 8:4-15)? This is not to underplay the significance of the initial encounter with Christ, but it is to stress that this encounter must bear fruit in a Christian life or else it contributes not to our salvation but to our condemnation.

It should be recognized that not all preaching in the church will be exclusively evangelistic. Christians need not only to repent but also to act upon their faith and learn more about it. There is certainly a place for teaching or instruction also in the proclamation of the church, but it should always be in the context of the evangel. In facing the world, however, the church

---

19 Jonathan Edwards, Edwards' "Miscellanies" Journal, Yale Collection (Yale Beinecke Rare Book and Manuscript Library), no. 996.

must rely only upon the Gospel message of salvation, for it alone arouses faith and brings men into the kingdom.

It is a serious error, in our estimation, to equate evangelism with social action or social service. *Diakonia* and *kerygma* are related, but they are not identical. All truly biblical preaching will have political implications and will bear fruit in social concern. Yet we should not preach politics as such, for the sermon is not a moral lecture on social problems. Nor should we simply by charitable acts of good will seek to win members to the church. Social reform is not the mission of the church although it may very well be a fruit and consequence of this mission. That evangelism has priority over social action in the life of the church can be seen in Ac. 6:1-5 where deacons were appointed to look after the social and material needs of the Christian community so that the apostles might be freed for full-time evangelistic work. We concur in the judgment of P. T. Forsyth:

> We are interested, of course, in the *amelioration* of society; and much is gained for its amelioration that we are so. But what society radically needs is *salvation;* and it is salvation that the Church offers to all. The Church alone has this secret — the Church, the greatest product of man's past, and the only trustee of his future.[20]

The error in the older revivalism is that conversion will automatically result in a better society. This would be true only if Christians were perfected men, but insofar as they remain sinners they too need to be restrained by the discipline of civil law. The error in the evangelistic strategy of secular theology is that a new society can be attained apart from converted men. There is here a failure to recognize that conversion entails an ontological change, that the convert is now a new creature (II Cor. 5:17).

The authority in a biblically based evangelism should be none other than the Word of God in Holy Scripture. God to be sure continues to speak and act today, but His speaking must be measured in the light of the biblical revelation which was given once for all times. The locus of revelation is not events of social change but the sacred history mirrored in the Bible. This revelation must be distinguished from the inspired record and witness to it or else we are prone to fall into a fundamentalistic literalism and biblicism. At the same time unless we acknowledge that the inspired text in Scripture is the focal point and vehicle of

---

20 P. T. Forsyth, *The Church and the Sacraments* (London: Independent Press, 1947), p. 6.

the revelation, we are likely to fall into the error of an exis-
tentialist subjectivism or mysticism.

The arena of salvation in a theology rooted in the Bible and
the Evangelical Reformation is not the present struggle for
social justice but rather the daily crisis of repentance and faith.
A life of penitence and faith will entail participation in the
struggle against racial discrimination and other social evils;
yet this struggle will be carried on with motivations and goals
quite different from those of the natural or secular man. Our
aim is not to build the open city of man (cf. Colin Williams)
but rather to point men to the kingdom that is not of this world.

Evangelism brings to men the opportunity for salvation and
not simply the knowledge of a salvation already procured for all
men in Jesus Christ (as Barthian theology generally alleges).
The life and death of Jesus Christ are the foundation and objective reality of our salvation, but salvation cannot be said to have
become a concrete reality in the lives of men until the fruits of
His sacrifice have been appropriated in repentance and faith.
The gates of the prison have been opened by the atoning work
of Christ, but we cannot be said "to be saved" unless we pass
through these gates into the full dispensation of Christian freedom.

Against the secular theologians we maintain that salvation is
not the same as humanization or rehabilitation. Divine justification must not be reduced to the forgiving and accepting love
which we experience in human relationships. Catharsis in the
psychological sense is surely not to be equated with regeneration or sanctification. Salvation means to be restored to a right
relationship with the holy God. It means that we have been
delivered not from oppression and persecution in this world
but rather from divine condemnation and hell.

Evangelism should also be clearly distinguished from apologetics. Our task is not to make the faith palatable to its cultured
despisers but to call people to repentance. We are not to answer
the creative questions of the secular culture but to confront this
culture with a definite message. According to Pascal, the apostle
did not appeal to wisdom and signs, "for he came to convert.
But those who come only to convince, can say that they come
with wisdom and signs."[21]

Biblical evangelism is founded on the truths that the Holy
Spirit is the only point of contact with the natural man and that

---

[21] Blaise Pascal, *Pascal's Pensées and the Provincial Letters,* trans. W. F.
Trotter and Thomas M'Crie (N.Y.: Modern Library, 1941), p. 192.

the Spirit has chosen to act through the preaching of the cross. This is why both the "Are you saved?" and "Are you in despair?" approaches are in error. We cannot appeal to any common understanding of salvation or any universal sense of guilt, since our hearers are not free to respond to the offer of salvation. They are made free by the Spirit when they hear the glad tidings of God's infinite love revealed in Jesus Christ, but this is no longer free will (*liberum arbitrium*) but rather a "liberated will" (*liberatum arbitrium*) brought into existence by free grace.

Because the natural man is in flight from God rather than in quest for God, because his will is bound and not free, evangelism should be carefully distinguished from dialogue. Dialogue is sometimes necessary in order to acquaint the church with the thought world and the problems of the secular man, but it does not of itself bring him one step nearer to salvation. It makes for congeniality but not conversion. Indeed, there can be no meaningful dialogue unless both sides stand upon common ground, but there is no common ground between faith and unbelief. In the light of Kierkegaard's insights, Everett Parker gives us this interpretation of the situation that confronts the herald of the Gospel: "The evangelist is not dealing with an uninformed person in need of information, nor with one who thirsts after knowledge, but with an anxious person running away from truth."[22] The aim of evangelism is neither mutual understanding nor togetherness nor a higher synthesis but rather surrender and commitment to the living Lord and Savior Jesus Christ. John Wesley said quite simply, "I offered Christ to the people," and this indeed is the hallmark of evangelistic preaching.

At the same time we must bear in mind that the word that we proclaim should be integrally related to the situation, both existential and cultural. We cannot make the Word of God knowable, but we can make it intelligible (Barth). It is incumbent upon us to proclaim this Word in the language of our hearers and to bring the specific sins of our society under the judgment of the Word. We are not called to mouth clichés but rather to present a coherent and compelling witness to the truth. Our task is not to preach the simple Gospel of the old time religion but the full Gospel of reconciliation and redemption which brings even our religion under judgment.

We need to take care also to distinguish biblical evangelism from proselytism. The latter might be defined as the attempt

---

[22] Everett C. Parker, "Christian Communication and Secular Man" in *The Ecumenical Review*, Vol. XVIII, No. 3 (July, 1966), (pp. 331-344), p. 335.

to win someone over to a doctrinal position or particular church. Its method is bringing pressure upon people, seeking to bend them in a particular direction. There can be no forcing of the truth upon men but rather simply sharing our faith with them in love. Evangelism is not a recruitment program for a particular church. Nor is it manipulation, treating people as objects. True evangelism is motivated by a love for persons as well as a zeal for the truth.

Evangelism springs from Christian life. The Word must always be related to the deed of self-giving love. Indeed, the Christian life can also be a means of grace when it is related to and grounded in the Christian Gospel (cf. Rom. 15:18; I Pt. 2:12). Yet life by itself cannot bring to men the word of forgiveness that they so desperately need to hear. As our Lord reminded us: "Man shall not live by bread alone, but by every word that proceeds from the mouth of God" (Mt. 4:4).

Evangelism should rise out of and lead into Christian fellowship. This is why we must speak of *koinonia* (fellowship) as well as *kerygma* and *diakonia*. Such groups as the Lee Abbey community and the Oxford Group movement have sought to expose men to the love of Christ by first introducing them to the fellowship of love. This form of missionary activity has been aptly called "fellowship evangelism," and we have no quarrel with this method so long as men are exposed to the Christian message as well. The bane of mass evangelism is that many converts are not introduced to a churchly fellowship where their faith can take root and grow. The decision for Christ cannot bear fruit apart from the church, the living community of faith, and this is why evangelists such as Billy Graham emphasize the necessity for church affiliation. What we should realize is that such affiliation is not simply a by-product of conversion but the necessary means for the full realization of conversion.

All Christians share in the evangelistic outreach of the church. But we hold that evangelistic preaching is a special charism. Every ordained minister must be in some sense an evangelist, but the charism of evangelism is manifest only in some people, whether they be ministers or laymen. This is why we believe that there is a place for an ordination to the office of an evangelist. We also would not be opposed to special evangelistic meetings in the church at certain times of the year where people might be given the opportunity to make a concrete and public profession of faith. Such meetings might well be related to the sacrament of Holy Communion, since repentance and decision are the conditions for participation in the sacrament. It is well to note that many of the early revivals on the American frontier began as services of preparation for Holy Communion.

If biblical evangelism is to be recovered in the church, we need to rediscover the truth that the goal of evangelical preaching is the glorification of God through the regeneration of sinners. Regeneration, moreover, signifies not merely reorientation but the washing away of sin. It effects not just a change of attitude but rather a new existence. This is what moved St. Paul to proclaim: "I have become all things to all men, that I might by all means save some" (I Cor. 9:22; Jude 22, 23; Jms. 5:20). This is what impelled Zinzendorf to declare: "My joy until I die: to win souls for the Lamb." The ills that afflict mankind can never begin to be solved until we have new men, men no longer motivated by pride and vain ambition but rather by sacrificial love and a burning passion for the lost. A secular journal has declared: "The pathology of racism is beyond the control of merely civil law. The cure for this debilitating disease lies in a spiritual renewal, a recognition of the equal worth of every person, of whatever color."[23] Such a recognition is only possible where the love of Jesus Christ controls and directs the actions of men. Surely the goal of evangelism is to bring to men this very love which alone can build the foundations of a relatively just society.

---

23 See *The Progressive,* Vol. 31, No. 9 (Sept., 1967), p. 9.

TWELVE:

# SPIRITUAL DISCIPLINES

### THE LOST DIMENSION IN PROTESTANTISM

The lack of vitality in modern Protestantism is at least partly to be attributed to the abysmal state of its spiritual life. The disciplines of the interior life can be regarded as the lost dimension in Protestantism today.[1] It is the outer world, not the inner life, that is considered the legitimate object of Christian concern. Man can be related to his God only by means of his neighbor, so many theologians contend; the possibility of personal, solitary communion with God is thereby denied. According to J. A. T. Robinson prayer is not "withdrawal from the world to God" but rather "penetration through the world to God." In his theology there is no longer a vertical relationship between God and man but only a horizontal relationship between man and his neighbor. The biblical distinction between the holy and the profane is not acknowledged by most contemporary theologians; service to the world has become our worship and prayer.

It is well to remember that the Protestant Reformers Luther and Calvin although protesting against the elevation of the religious above the common life nevertheless held to the basic distinction between the Holy and the profane. Indeed, it can be said that they heightened this distinction, since they identified the Holy with the transcendent God who towers above and judges both the religious and the secular. They also drew sharp lines of demarcation between the adoration of God and service to one's fellowmen, in contrast to many of the Catholic mystics. Luther defined adoration as an acknowledgment of the benefits of God in prayer, thanksgiving and the hearing of the sermon; service on the other hand is an act of kindness towards our neighbor. In adoration we surrender to God and receive from God. In service we do a good work; therefore service be-

---

[1] See the chapter "Toward the Recovery of the Devotional Life" in Donald G. Bloesch, *The Crisis of Piety* (Grand Rapids: Eerdmans, 1968), pp. 63-76.

longs in the realm of law whereas adoration is to be related to the Gospel.[2]

Perhaps in their fear of works-righteousness the Reformers were not sufficiently cognizant of the truth that the spiritual life also entails works, to be sure of a different character from the works of the law. The spiritual life, i.e., the life of adoration and personal faith, cannot maintain itself apart from spiritual disciplines and exercises. The Anabaptists accented the disciplines of the Christian life, but they thereby incurred the reproach of the Reformers that they were reverting to medieval Catholicism. The post-Reformation movements of Pietism and Puritanism perceived the need for the disciplined life of devotion more clearly than the Reformation itself, and indeed these movements signalized the flowering of an evangelical spiritual life.[3] The guiding lights of these movements were generally very much aware of the dangers of legalism and moralism by which the Christian life is viewed as a means of gaining justification or meriting divine favor. They also sought to guard against Pharisaism by recognizing the truth that the Christian is a sinner and thereby remains in constant need of divine forgiveness. Yet it cannot be denied that in later evangelical revivalism these perils became very real and the Reformation message of justification by free grace was partially obscured.

If spiritual disciplines have been misused in Roman Catholicism and pietistic Protestantism, they have been sorely neglected in the mainstream of modern Protestantism. Surely one reason for this is the widespread reaction to an unbalanced emphasis on these disciplines in the older pietism. Spiritual disciplines too often remind people today of the moralism and rigorism associated with an otherworldly asceticism. The mood of the modern age also goes counter to the biblical themes of self-denial and self-sacrifice. Even Schleiermacher, who sought to make a place for the interior life, nevertheless looked askance upon spiritual exercises and outward disciplines.

> Spare me the long catalogue of outward disciplines, spiritual exercises, privations, mortifications and the rest. All these things you accuse religion of producing, and yet you cannot overlook the fact that the greatest heroes of religion, the founders and

---

[2] Martin Luther, *Table Talk*, Vol. 54 in *Luther's Works*, trans. and ed. Theodore G. Tappert (Philadelphia: Fortress, 1967), p. 102.

[3] See F. Ernest Stoeffler, *The Rise of Evangelical Pietism* (Leiden: E. J. Brill, 1965); and Gordon Wakefield, *Puritan Devotion* (London: Epworth Press, 1957).

reformers of the church, have regarded them with great indifference.[4]

It is true that the radical mystics have treated spiritual disciplines with indifference, and yet the prophets and evangelical
reformers although not regarding such disciplines as necessary
for salvation have nevertheless stressed their practical value for
Christian living.

Liberal Protestantism has generally regarded the attempts at
spiritual discipline with disfavor. Ritschlian theology perceived
the essence of Christianity to lie in ethical obedience. The theology emanating from Schleiermacher placed the stress on religious
experience rather than spiritual exercises. The Social Gospel
movement and the new Social Gospel of secular theology uphold
social righteousness but have very little to say about personal
conversion and sanctification.

The neo-orthodox theology associated with Barth, Brunner
and Reinhold Niebuhr has sought to revive the Reformation
doctrine of the justification of the ungodly. But when justification as well as sanctification is viewed as something that happens
wholly outside of us as in Barthian theology, the disciplines
of the spiritual life cease to have decisive significance. Moreover,
the neo-orthodox emphasis upon the continuing sinfulness of
the Christian cuts the nerve out from any attempt to discipline
oneself morally and spiritually. Mention should also be made
of the view commonly advanced in Barthian circles that revelation signifies the negation or even the abolition of human
religion. It is not surprising that very little if anything has been
written in neo-orthodox theology about the need for the recovery
of the disciplines of devotion.

The inner or spiritual life is particularly under eclipse in
American Protestantism, since the hallmark of our culture is
other-direction rather than inner-direction (Riesmann). Our
ideals and values are derived more from the dictates of the
culture than from the inner voice of conscience or the spiritual
light within. Our churches are still prospering, but we have
to ask how much we have lost. Our people are busy in church
work and worthwhile community activities, and yet they lack
an inner purpose and direction. Modern Protestants, particularly
American Protestants, are not anchored in anything eternal and
substantial because they have not cultivated and nurtured an
inner relationship and communion with divine reality. Their

---

4 Friedrich Schleiermacher, *On Religion,* trans. John Oman (N.Y.: Harper
Torchbooks, 1965), p. 60.

social life is over-abundant, but their spiritual life is practically nil. We have expanded the organization, but we have lost our soul in the process. Surely a crying need of our time is the recovery of the interior life of devotion.

## THE SPIRITUALLY DISCIPLINED LIFE

Among the disciplines that are indispensable for the life of devotion is prayer. And yet many Christians today, including theologians, openly acknowledge that their prayer life is virtually nonexistent. In some quarters prayer is being drastically reinterpreted to signify a reflection upon the needs of our fellowmen and then rising to meet these needs. But this is no longer prayer but meditation, and the kind that has man rather than God as its object. Prayer cannot become a living reality in the lives of men unless it is recognized as being essentially supplication to a personal God who is capable of accomplishing what is requested. Prayer in the mind of the Bible consists in the pouring out of the soul before God, not in a mystical contemplation of the being of God. There is a need for an evangelical meditation directed to the passion and victory of Christ, but it should not be regarded as authentic prayer. Prayer consists not only in direct petition but also in adoration, thanksgiving and confession, but all of these forms can be shown to be variants of petitionary prayer.

A word should also be said about aids to prayer. Posture can be very important in helping one to pray. Calvin recommended kneeling for private prayer. The early Christians often stood for prayer with arms extended toward heaven. Symbols such as the crucifix can be powerful aids in enabling one to concentrate upon the object of prayer. Symbolic acts such as the sign of the cross can prepare one to enter into conversation with God. The reading of psalms before or after prayer can serve to strengthen the prayer life. The singing of hymns in connection with the act of prayer can also be of much help. Set times for prayers are also to be encouraged, since although one can pray at any time he is more likely to do so at times that are set aside for this purpose.

Study is also a spiritual discipline that is not to be ignored. So often study is associated with purely academic pursuits, but the study of the Bible and of devotional classics is a spiritual exercise as well. Yet a disciplined study of the sources of faith and piety is definitely neglected in the modern church. The biblical illiteracy of even teachers in Sunday Schools is something to be deplored. Most ministers although having a technical familiarity with the Bible are not really searching the Scriptures for the will and purpose of God concerning the life of their congregation and their own devotional life. This is why for the most part people are not hearing the Word of God from the pulpit. Both pastors and laymen need to impose upon themselves the discipline of the daily study of Scripture and of other works of a spiritual and theological character if they are to have a zeal informed by knowledge.

Simplicity is also a hallmark of the spiritually disciplined life. In a time when material affluence is considered the badge of respectability and the goal in life, we need to be reminded that the Christian style of life entails the sacrifice of the goods of life for the sake of the kingdom of God. To be sure the sacrifice that most Christians are called to make is the inward one. We are to be inwardly detached from material things, but we are permitted, even commanded, as stewards to use these things for the glory of God. Simplicity does not necessarily mean poverty, since we may use unrighteous mammon for worthy purposes (Lk. 16:9). At the same time there is a difference between living in luxury and living an abundant life that is dedicated to the welfare of others. Too often there is the temptation to accumulate the goods of life and refuse to share with others. Christians who seek the most expensive car or the most luxurious home are surely often motivated by the desire to keep up with the Joneses; we tend to forget that we can serve the cause of Christ just as easily with a more modest car and home. The same can be said for wearing apparel which more often than not reflects the latest style or rage rather than Christian simplicity. Simplicity, however, should not be confused with a severity or barrenness that more often than not is a form of spiritual exhibitionism.

In this connection it is appropriate to consider the discipline of fasting. In a time when people particularly in our Western society are overeating and when the majority of people in the world are in dire need of food, the spiritual exercise of fasting can again be recommended. A newspaper item stated that per capita beef consumption rose from 59.4 lbs. to 99.3 lbs. within a recent ten-year period. A TV advertisement declares that when one has stuffed himself to the limit he can still find room for jello. We have not yet approached the excessive debauchery of the Roman Empire in its last days when people left the banquet halls to vomit and then returned again to gorge themselves.

Yet we need to take seriously the fact that gluttony was num-
bered among the seven deadly sins by medieval theologians.
Luther made this trenchant criticism:

> ...gluttony and drunkenness are the fertile soil in which
> unchastity or debauchery thrive. For this reason the pious
> Fathers declared that whoever desires to serve God, must root
> out, above all, the vice of gluttony. That is a prevailing vice
> which causes much trouble. If this vice is not altogether extir-
> pated, it makes the soul dull for divine things, even if it should
> not lead to unchastity and debauchery as among aged men.
> Hence fasting is a most excellent weapon for the Christian,
> while gluttony is an outstanding pit of Satan.[5]

Fasting can be recommended for the Christian, but it must be
rightly understood if it is not to become a tool of legalism. First
of all fasting should be seen as a private rather than a public
exercise (Mt. 6:16-18). Again, it should be viewed as a voluntary
and not a compulsory discipline. Luther spoke about the value
of fasting during Holy Week, but he hastened to add, "Not
that we compel anyone to fast. . . ." St. Paul recommended periods
of fasting (in the sexual sphere) for husbands and wives, but
he made clear that this was a personal suggestion rather than a
spiritual mandate (I Cor. 7:5). When fasting is made into a
norm or rule, then it no longer can be viewed as an act of piety.
But it should be encouraged as a means of drawing closer to
God in prayer. It is also a poignant reminder of the starvation
and misery in the world.

Surely chastity is another discipline of the spiritual life that
needs to be given special emphasis today. In a culture where the
suppression of sexual appetite is generally regarded as the pathway to neurosis, the church has been under increasing pressure
to relax the moral standards that have guided it in the past.
Some theologians are now questioning the traditional ban upon
premarital and extramarital relations as well as advocating trial
marriages. It is becoming commonplace in most avant garde
theological circles to depict homosexuality as a weakness for
which the subject is not responsible rather than as a sin before
God. Proponents of the new morality view it as a medical rather
than a moral problem. Christians today need to heed the warning of Scripture that adulterers, fornicators, homosexuals and
drunkards will be barred from the kingdom of heaven (I Cor.
6:9, 10; Rev. 21:8).

In the Christian view sex is both a gift of God and a potential

---

[5] Martin Luther, *Commentary on the Epistle to the Romans*, trans. J.
Theodore Mueller (Grand Rapids: Zondervan, 1954), p. 175.

instrument of human lust. Because it is a part of God's creation it should be accepted rather than repudiated. But inasmuch as it is tainted by human sin, it should be restrained and channeled by both law and grace. In Christian ethics sexual relations are permissible only within the state of holy matrimony and even then our sexual life needs constantly to be covered by divine forgiveness. Apart from marriage the Christian ideal is absti- nence from the sexual act, and through divine grace this ideal can actually be realized. Celibacy has from the New Testament on occupied an important place in Christian spirituality and has generally been regarded with marriage as a way to holiness. Yet Christians fell into error when they began to view celi- bacy as having greater merit or worth than marriage. The Protestant Reformation reminded the church that marriage in the Lord is also a pathway to sanctity. Celibacy can be seen to have a practical but not a moral advantage over marriage. Chastity should not be identified with celibacy, since Chris- tians in the married state are also called to discipline their passions. Man in his fallen state is naturally polygamous, and this means that the Christian whether married or single is called to a life of spiritual heroism.

Finally it is well to consider the discipline of participation in the services and fellowship of the church. Against the individual- ism that has marred evangelical piety in the past we contend that no man can be a Christian alone. He needs the guidance and support of the fellowship of believers which is the church. Church participation is important because it is in the fellowship of believers that we hear the Word of God and partake of the sacraments. The spiritual masters remind us that the Christian life can be maintained only by constant contact with the Word and sacraments. To be sure if the worship service is no longer centered about the Word and if the sacrament of Holy Com- munion is celebrated only once or twice a year, then the spiritual life of the Christian is placed in jeopardy. But we would then add that the church has ceased to exist, and Christians must seek some other fellowship where the Word is being proclaimed and faithfully expounded and where the sacrament is made available to the people. As a rule the Christian should remain in his own church and seek to reform it particularly if the Gospel is still present whether in the preaching or the liturgy. On the other hand, when the world has so penetrated the life of the church that the Gospel itself is no longer in view, then

Christians have an obligation to withdraw from what is now a social club and rejoin the community of the Word.

Much could be said of other spiritual disciplines including silence, early rising, the reading of Scripture, abstinence from wine and tobacco, hospitality and Sabbath observance. What should be noted is that not every spiritual exercise is particularly suitable for all Christians. There is need for much experimentation in the area of spiritual disciplines and aids to devotion. Generally speaking when a particular discipline has outlived its usefulness, then it should be discarded. Some disciplines of the spirit can never be abandoned, however, without jeopardizing the Christian life itself. Among these are prayer, the reading and hearing of the Word of God, liberality and chastity.

## TOWARDS THE RECOVERY OF THE SPIRITUAL LIFE

One of the principal needs today is the recovery of theological foundations for a life of devotion. A dualistic asceticism on the one hand and a spiritualistic individualism on the other have placed the spiritual life under the shadow of heresy. It is no secret that the majority of popular books on prayer and devotion today have little if any biblical and theological substance. Unless the disciplined life of devotion is anchored in an objective historical revelation, it becomes susceptible to the fantasies and extravagances of the religious imagination.

First it is necessary to understand that the devotional life is not a way to salvation, as in Bhakti Hinduism for example, but rather a sign and fruition of salvation. The disciplines of the spirit do not save us in the sense of earning for us divine justification. Rather they are the consequence and evidence of the justification procured for us by Jesus Christ on the cross of Calvary. They are practical ways of strengthening our fellowship with God, but not means of meriting His favor. At the same time it should be recognized that the disciplines of the spirit serve to keep us on the way to salvation even though they cannot set us on the way. We cannot win our salvation through such disciplines, but apart from these disciplines we can lose the benefits of salvation. The disciplines of the spiritual life are also means to the salvation of others. We concur in the judgment of Philip Spener that "holiness of life itself contributes much to [the] conversion" of our fellowman.[6]

The motivation for living the life of devotion should be

---

[6] Philip Jacob Spener, *Pia Desideria,* trans. and ed. Theodore G. Tappert (Philadelphia: Fortress, 1964), p. 102.

primarily the glorification of God. At the same time there are secondary motivations that can be made to serve the glory of God, such as gratefulness for the gift of Christ, the fear of God and the desire for salvation. Some theologians argue that the latter two motivations are unworthy of the spiritual man, and yet they are solidly Scriptural. They become dangerous only if they are divorced from the desire to give all the glory to God.

A dualistic asceticism stemming from Neo-Platonism and Manichaeism and entering into Christian thought by way of the Christian mystics has served to undermine the evangelical foundations of the spiritual life as given in the Bible. According to this kind of asceticism, the antithesis is between spirit and nature rather than between the holy God and man the sinner. In the religion of mysticism the goal of man is to extricate himself from the bonds of the flesh so that his soul might be reunited with its divine ground. The mystical ideal is the "flight of the alone to the alone" (Plotinus) rather than fellowship with God and neighbor. The Protestant Reformers and many evangelicals within Roman Catholicism have warned of the perils of this kind of spirituality. They remind us of Paul's admonition to nourish and cherish our bodies (Eph. 5:29). The hallmark of authentic Christian spirituality is not world-denial but self-denial. What we should seek for is not holy solitariness but social holiness (Wesley).

Yet too often we as Protestants are inclined to view the heritage of Christian mysticism only in negative terms; our eyes are closed to the authentic biblical and evangelical elements which this heritage contains. Many of the Christian mystics were also aware of the pitfalls of a dualistic ascetic spirituality. Against the Platonizers they often pointed to the truth that the seat of sin is not in the body but in the heart of man. Meister Eckhart could even make the statement that the body was given to purify the soul. Francis of Assisi, who referred to his body as "Brother Ass," perceived the truth that the body is the medium or instrument of the inner self rather than a prison. In Fénelon's view it is incumbent upon one not only to renounce the body but also the soul. Catherine of Siena averred: "Perfection does not consist in macerating or killing the body, but in killing our perverse self-will." Francis de Sales was convinced of the need to purify the soul, although he also held that the soul is eternal and worthy of eternity.[7] The mystical ideal is a spiritual marriage of the soul with God, and yet many of the mystics also alluded to spiritual fecundity which consists in sharing the faith with others.[8] Eckhart reflects this point of view when he affirms, "What a man takes in in contemplation, he must pour out in love." That the mystics were not wholly successful in maintaining an evangelical stance must not blind us to the genuinely biblical motifs in their thinking. It should also be recognized that they retained certain biblical truths that have been lost sight of in Protestantism, such as the necessity for a certain degree of solitude and silence in prayer and the need for frequent participation in the blessed sacrament.

Modern Protestantism is in crisis today partly because we have lost the disciplines of the spirit. Walter Wagoner has noted that Protestant seminaries have become almost purely academic instead of centers of faith and piety.[9] Wayne Oates has complained that "the curriculum and the economic pressures under which students and faculty work leave little room or opportunity for the small group exploration of the personal religious life of both students and faculty."[10] As we draw closer to our Roman Catholic and Eastern Orthodox brethren we as Protestants should come to appreciate the vision of the monastery, the place of retreat, which has enabled countless thousands to fortify themselves spiritually for the purpose of mission and service in the world. What we tend to forget is that there can be no profound and lasting penetration into the secular world apart from periodic withdrawal from the world. We have so emphasized the virtue of work that we have forgotten the need for silence and meditation, and thereby our work has become empty and meaningless. Most modern Christians have busily immersed themselves in church and community activities but have lost sight of their spiritual goals. Busy work can often be a means of escape not only from ourselves but also from God. The mystics

---

[7] Francis de Sales, *Introduction to the Devout Life*, trans. and ed. John K. Ryan (London: Longmans, Green, 1953), pp. 12, 13, 191, 319.

[8] See Dom Cuthbert Butler, *Western Mysticism* (N.Y.: Harper Torchbooks, 1966), pp. 113, 195, 208, 211.

[9] Walter Wagoner, "Winds and Windmills: a Weather Report on Seminary Education in the USA" in *Bulletin of the Department of Theology of the World Alliance of Reformed Churches* (Summer, 1966), Vol. 6, No. 4, p. 6. See also Walter Wagoner, *The Seminary Protestant and Catholic* (N.Y.: Sheed & Ward, 1966).

[10] Frank Stagg, E. Glenn Hinson and Wayne E. Oates, *Glossolalia: Tongue Speaking in Biblical, Historical, and Psychological Perspective* (Nashville: Abingdon, 1968), p. 82.

remind us of the necessity for detachment from the world of things if we are to find both God and ourselves. What are needed in modern Protestantism are retreats and training centers in Christian devotion that can serve as spiritual oases in the modern desert of secularism and nihilism. The disciplines of the spirit, which are now almost wholly neglected in our colleges and seminaries, would certainly be included in the curriculum of such centers or institutes. For apart from the disciplines, the inner or spiritual life of man will most surely die. The very existence of the church is then placed in jeopardy, since the power and purpose of the Christian mission will have been lost.

# THIRTEEN:

# THE NEED FOR SOCIAL RELEVANCE

Many people today are rejecting the Christian faith not only because of the scandal of the cross but also because of false stumbling blocks erected by Christians which keep men from confronting the cross. Among these is the reluctance of the church to condemn social evils by which God is blasphemed and His people are maligned and degraded. Reinhold Niebuhr has declared that it is not the incredibility of the faith so much as its social impotence that renders it suspect to intellectuals. We need today to rediscover the social relevance of the Gospel. Indeed, as John Mackay has aptly remarked, we are not only called to accept Jesus Christ as Savior but also to follow Him as Lord in active obedience.[1] And it is imperative that we acknowledge the lordship of Christ not simply in the private sphere of life but also in the public sphere, in the world of politics and economics.

## TWO DIMENSIONS OF THE CHRISTIAN LIFE

This brings us to the two sides of the Christian life. The first might be called the devotional which includes *latria* (worship), *kerygma* and *leitourgia*. Here we are concerned with the life of prayer and adoration. The second dimension of the Christian life is *diakonia* (service). Indeed, we are told not only to be hearers of the Word but doers as well (Jms. 1:22). This area of Christian life encompasses both charitable works and prophetic involvement. When we speak of social relevance, we have in mind the service of our neighbor in all its varied ramifications.

The call to a life of service is to be found throughout the Bible. We are urged in the Old Testament to care for orphans and widows (cf. Ex. 22:22; Mal. 3:5), a note which is also sounded in the New Testament (I Tim. 5:16; Jms. 1:27). Again,

[1] John A. Mackay, *His Life and Our Life* (Philadelphia: Westminster, 1964), pp. 11, 12.

it is said that the children of Israel should have a loving concern
for the hungry, the naked and the homeless poor (Is. 58:6, 7).
The demand of the law was to feed poor people and strangers
by leaving a strip of crops in the fields for their use. In the New
Testament the accent was placed upon compassion for the sick,
the hungry, the oppressed and the outcasts of society. The
Scriptures remind us that the church should not only be concerned with changing man's nature but also with improving
man's lot. We should recognize that Jesus not only preached the
Gospel, but He also healed the sick and fed the hungry. Indeed,
if we are not Good Samaritans as well as heralds, our witness is
abstract and self-defeating. In the parable of the last judgment
(Mt. 25) it is made clear that the criterion for the acceptance
or rejection of men lies in the fruits of their faith, in whether
they feed the hungry, clothe the naked, or visit the sick and those
in prison.

It is well to recognize that service entails more than charity.
It also includes social action, i.e., the application of power on
the part of Christians to change social conditions. Too often
Christians, and Protestants in particular, have expended their
energies upon caring for the victims of social injustice rather
than seeking to improve the social environment which breeds
injustice. The Old Testament prophets did not hesitate to
summon the rulers of their nation and of other nations to
correct social inequities. Amos condemned various nations of
his time for their immoral methods in waging warfare (Am.
1, 2). He castigated the landowners of Israel for trampling
upon the poor and exacting wheat from them (Am. 2:6, 7; 5:11).
Daniel called upon King Nebuchadnezzar to "break off your
sins by practicing righteousness, and your iniquities by showing mercy to the oppressed" (Dan. 4:27). For the prophets
faith in God means more than trust and confidence; it entails
obedience to God in all areas of life.

The older evangelicals were not averse to social action so
long as it served not clerical control but the correction of grave
social abuses. It is well to note that evangelicals, who accentuated
the life of prayer and devotion, comprised the main arm of
the movement for the abolition of slavery in both England and
America. It has also been evangelical Christians who have been
chiefly responsible for securing legislation designed to control
gambling, pornography, dope peddling and alcoholism. Calvin
upheld the ideal of a "holy community" in which every area of
life would be under the rule of divine law; his Puritan followers

sought to create "holy commonwealths" with the same purpose in mind. Wesley inveighed against what he termed "holy solitaries" and reminded the Christians of his time that the biblical ideal is "social holiness."

## MORAL ISSUES OF OUR TIME

We must now ask ourselves what kinds of issues and problems in society should claim the serious attention of the church. When do secular controversies assume a moral and even spiritual dimension so that the church is impelled to speak out even if this opens it to the charge of meddling in politics? Surely the church must prepare itself for active confrontation with the culture when obedience to God is at stake. Spiritual issues are those that concern not simply our relationship to our neighbor but our relationship to God. They are issues which drive us to action out of spiritual conviction and not simply out of social concern. They are in other words matters of faith and not simply matters of sociology, politics or economics. Unfortunately many churches have seen fit to address themselves to problems in which the moral implications are not at all clear. Moreover, these same bodies also seek to give political advice rather than bring the problem under the scrutiny of the Word of God. Whether Red China should be admitted to the United Nations; whether America should resume diplomatic and trade relations with Cuba; or whether the voting age should be lowered to eighteen are not questions on which the church can speak with an authoritative voice. The church must take care never to confuse politics and morality even though the two cannot finally be separated.

The church is not to engage in partisan politics but rather to uphold the Word of God. It is not to proclaim a Social Gospel but instead the Gospel of the cross. Yet this Gospel has social and even political implications. This is why a sermon if directed to the social situation in which men live will border on the political and may even assume a political coloration. Karl Barth has gone so far as to declare: "It is a bad sign when Christians are frightened by 'political' sermons — as if Christian preaching could be anything but political. And if it were not political, how would it show that it is the salt and the light of the world?"[2] Barth does not believe, however, that the church should derive its measure of judgment from the world

---

[2] Karl Barth, *Community, State and Church* (Garden City, N.Y.: Doubleday, 1960), p. 185.

of politics or that it should look to that world for the final answer to the problems that afflict men. But in addressing ourselves to the world we also necessarily address ourselves to the political life of men, and sometimes this will involve us in criticisms and pronouncements of a political nature.

Berdyaev has made the cogent observation that bread for oneself is a material problem but bread for other people is a spiritual problem. Whenever men are being deprived of human dignity and the means of livelihood, God's commandment "Thou shalt not kill" is being abrogated. As the Book of Sirach affirms, "The bread of the needy is the life of the poor; whoever deprives them of it is a man of blood. To take away a neighbor's living is to murder him, to deprive an employee of his wages is to shed blood" (34:21, 22). Whenever men arrogate to themselves supreme power and demand from others slavish obedience, the sovereignty of God and the lordship of Christ are being denied. Whenever men exploit their fellowmen, they are transgressing the commandments against stealing and covetousness. Here again we contend that it is God's Word and not simply the plight of our fellowmen that calls us to obedience in the political sphere of life.

Surely racial hatred and discrimination contravene the Scriptural truth that all men are created in the image of God and that all have fallen from their divine estate. Racism also calls into question the central message of the Bible that Jesus Christ died for all men. The principle of human brotherhood is not the inherent infinite worth of the human soul but the universal claim of Christian redemption. Our motivation to service is not simply respect for human personality but gratefulness for God's outpoured love in Jesus Christ. We are called as Christians not merely to tolerance and mutual goodwill but to an infinite preference for our neighbor's welfare. The ideal in human relations is forgiving and accepting love, and yet when our fellowmen are denied human dignity, it is then incumbent upon us to unite love with power and seek to redress social wrongs. Civil laws cannot make bad people good, but they can make innocent people safe (Martin Luther King). When human rights conflict with property rights, we aver that human rights take precedence; therefore Christians should fervently support laws for open housing both at the state and federal levels.

The breakdown in sexual morality is another area that the church cannot ignore if it is to uphold the law of God as well as the Gospel. It is our view that the church should take a definite stand against sexual promiscuity and perversion and also against the new morality which seeks to accommodate Christian moral standards to the prevailing mores of our time. It must act upon this problem out of a concern to protect our youth from exploitation and to safeguard the body which is the temple of God. The churches need once again to uphold the ideal of chastity in the face of a widespread and growing contempt for the virtues of marital fidelity and premarital virginity. Sex can be a blessing when it is controlled and directed by Christian love, but it can become a curse when it serves self-gratification and the lust for power.

The gravest moral issue of our time, according to Karl Barth, is the nuclear bomb, weapons of mass extermination. If the church is to maintain its integrity in our day, it must declare that such weapons are an abomination in the sight of God. Indeed, these are arms that not only can destroy an attacking enemy but also kill and maim millions of innocent bystanders including women and children, even those yet unborn. Indeed, the use of such weapons would disfigure nature itself and would render large areas of the globe uninhabitable. There is indeed a qualitative difference between weapons of mass extermination (whether nuclear, chemical or biological) and conventional weaponry such as swords, guns and even pin-point bombing. Nuclear warfare can only be validly compared to saturation or obliteration bombing which occurred towards the close of the second world war and which destroyed whole cities as well as armaments industries and munitions centers. A few voices in the Christian world protested against the savagery and barbarism of saturation bombing, but our policy was to win by any means. Pope John has declared that in an atomic world the concept of a just war is passé. It is completely unrealistic to assume that a just war could ever be waged with weapons of mass extermination. A new kind of pacifism has now become a live option for many Christians, and the church should encourage its children to withhold their support from any armaments program that entails the use of these weapons. Surely even participation in the manufacture of such arms should be out of bounds for those who would be disciples of Christ. The churches must also warn their governments of the divine judgment that lies over the world because of the preparation for war with nuclear weapons and also because of man's idolatrous dependence upon these weapons. Christians should certainly support multilateral nuclear disarmament and a worldwide ban on nuclear testing.

Several years ago some members of the faculty of the Dubuque Theological Seminary issued a statement condemning the use of weapons of mass extermination in warfare. The following affirmations are particularly significant:

> There is ... no conceivable end that justifies these means — neither the salvation of the West with what is here called Christian civilization, nor the salvation of the East with what is there called the achievements of the socialist revolution.... All men and nations who follow the policy of war by mass extermination provoke the wrath of God and His just retribution, whether they deny Him or whether they profess their worship of Him.[3]

In this connection we must ask whether the church has the right to declare itself in opposition to the war in Vietnam. Various ecclesiastical bodies, including the World Council of Churches, have issued manifestos condemning the American war action in Vietnam as immoral. Some church leaders have even gone so far as to offer political directives to the various heads of governments on how to bring this war to an end. In our opinion the church should proceed with caution in this area because the issues are exceedingly complex, and vital information is very probably being withheld from the public. There is no clear-cut divine imperative that is easily discernible in this situation, and it should also be recognized that biblical faith does not deny to a nation the right to request outside aid in its defense against aggression. Granted that the government in South Vietnam was originally imposed by the United States upon the South Vietnamese, we must be careful not to confuse the prophetic role of the church with purely political considerations which are often outside its competence.

Without calling for unconditional withdrawal from Vietnam Christians can protest against the often immoral methods in waging warfare which our government has appeared to countenance, some of which are explicitly condemned in Scripture. The napalm bombing of open villages, the torturing of prisoners (by our allies the South Vietnamese) and the uprooting and herding of hundreds of thousands of homeless peasants into refugee camps are all to be deplored. Moreover, our government has admitted using "non-toxic" gas in Vietnam, but it contends that this weapon is a "humane" one because it creates only temporary nausea and diarrhea in adult victims. Yet a *New York Times* editorial on March 24, 1965, noted that these gases "can be

---

[3] See the statement *Mass Extermination as a Means of Waging War* (Dubuque Presbyterian Press, Jan. 12, 1960).

fatal to the very young, the very old, and those with heart and lung ailments. . . . No other country has employed such a weapon in recent warfare." We recognize the right of a nation to use force to preserve law and order, but we object to needless cruelty, to wanton killing. We concur in the judgment of Walter Stein, which would seem to apply to both sides in the Vietnamese conflict:

> . . . the objection to murdering non-combatants is not simply that it makes war a degree more horrible, but that it is wicked. The killing of combatants is indeed a necessary evil — something ghastly which we may find ourselves bound to do; the killing of non-combatants is a *moral* evil, something which we have never the right to do.[4]

In our protests against the government on the question of war or any other question, we must pay heed to the apostle's admonition that secular government is an order of creation and that we are required to respect and obey the authorities that God has placed over us (Rom. 13:1-7; Tit. 3:1, 2). There is no place in the Christian strategy for the burning of draft cards, the adulation of leaders of enemy nations, or the desecration of the national flag. Whether Christians can ever refuse to pay taxes is also questionable, although there may be exceptions particularly if tax money is being used almost entirely for immoral purposes. Yet we would do well to bear in mind the words of Jesus that tax money belongs to Caesar (Mt. 22:15-22). At the same time we are forbidden to give the state absolute loyalty, and when the state makes such a demand upon us then we can only testify as did the apostle, "We must obey God rather than men" (Ac. 5:29). The state can require from us our respect and loyalty, but it cannot demand from us participation in acts of murder and barbarism. Civil disobedience must never be carried to the point where the divinely given rights of the state itself are disregarded, because then we are on the verge of anarchy. But at the same time we are bound to resist the dictates of the state when these contradict the express will of God in Scripture.

While the threat of the mass extermination of peoples presents a grave problem, overpopulation is surely another moral and spiritual issue of our time. The church has an obligation to emphasize the biblical truth that we are now living in the dispensation of Christ and are no longer under the Old Testa-

---

4 G. E. M. Anscombe, et al., *Nuclear Weapons — A Catholic Response* (N.Y.: Sheed & Ward, 1961), p. 28.

ment command to be fruitful and multiply (cf. Gen. 1:22). Christ is now the symbol of fruitfulness, and the purpose of Christian families is to bring forth spiritual children. Families may still be permitted children of their own, but the accent should now be on the principle that these children belong first of all to Christ. Moreover, the very purpose of marriage should be seen as a partnership in kingdom service and not as biological fertility which is the emphasis in most pagan religions. Birth control should be encouraged, but not for selfish purposes but rather for the divine ends of service and evangelism. The church must warn, however, against the indiscriminate use of contraceptives and also the resort to abortion as a solution to the population problem. Pope Paul's encyclical *Humanae Vitae,* which categorically condemns all contraception, is in my opinion a step backward; yet this is not to deny that this encyclical mirrors a profound concern over the deterioration of morals in our time.

We could mention many other critical issues of our time that are basically spiritual and that must be included in the prophetic criticism of the church. Among these are alcoholism, water pollution, air pollution, the gambling craze and dope addiction. Mention might also be made of the new factory farms in which farm animals are reduced to machines and subjected to unwarranted stress and torture.[5] The church must take care not to open its mouth on every problem in society, since many problems are of a partisan political nature and the moral implications are not obvious. On the other hand, it dare not remain silent in the face of social evils that are clearly forbidden in Scripture and that contravene the divine law of love.

## SOCIAL ACTION

Granted that social evils exist, does the protest of the Christian entail social or political action as well as proclamation? Does the Christian have the right to use temporal power in addition to love in order to achieve justice? We contend that it is imperative that Christians as both churchmen and citizens enter the power structures of society in order to accomplish specific social objectives. Yet we believe that the church as a church should beware of becoming directly involved in the temporal power struggle, since its mission is essentially spiritual. It may

---

[5] See Donald G. Bloesch, "Intensive Farming" in *Lutheran Forum* (July 1968), Vol. 2, No. 7, pp. 4-6. Also see Ruth Harrison, *Animal Machines,* Foreword by Rachel Carson (N.Y.: Ballantine Books, 1966).

seem that we are introducing the two kingdom theory of Lutheranism, and yet it must be recognized that the church serves a
kingdom that is not of this world (Jn. 18:36). Too many times
in the past the church has made the mistake of seeking itself to
be a power structure and of trying to dominate the culture. Hans
Küng makes the poignant observation that one reason for the
failure of the Catholic church in Italy to stem the Communist
upsurge in that country is that it has too often sought to
advance itself through political means and has practically
abandoned its mission of preaching the Word of God.[6] Gayraud
Wilmore believes that the church has an obligation to use
power in another way.

> The responsibility of the church for power does not mean
> bidding for sovereignty over the structures and institutions of
> society. It means penetrating them in such a way as to be
> able to instruct the world concerning its purpose of serving
> human need, concerning its original foundation and the end
> toward which it moves.[7]

We hold that as a general rule it is churchmen but not
churches that should engage in political action. The duty of
the church is to stir the conscience of the community and thereby arouse men of good will to courageous action. As Paul
Ramsey has cogently stated in his *Who Speaks for the Church?*,
the church should point directions but refrain from issuing directives.[8] It should not be a maker of political policy, but it
should "nourish, judge and repair the moral and political
ethos." It should not seek to be a "little state" and offer blue-
prints on social policy, but its members as citizens of the state
should enter actively into the world of politics in order to bring
about needed corrections of social abuses.

What are the kinds of social action that are open to Christians? Surely boycotts are in order against restaurants or other
places of business that exploit their employees or blatantly
discriminate against members of minority races. Picketing is
another method of social action which can be used against any
place or agency which has become an instrument of injustice or

---

[6] Hans Küng, *Freedom Today*, trans. Cecily Hastings (N.Y.: Sheed &
Ward, 1966), pp. 169, 170.

[7] Gayraud S. Wilmore, *The Secular Relevance of the Church* (Philadelphia: Westminster, 1962), p. 59. We do not subscribe, however, to Wilmore's interpretation of the mission of the church as essentially secular
rather than spiritual.

[8] Paul Ramsey, *Who Speaks For the Church?* (Nashville: Abingdon,
1967).

idolatry. The civil rights marches and peace marches may also be legitimate ways for Christians to proclaim their grievances. Letters to the editor of the daily newspaper and also to representatives and senators in Washington are another means by which social pressure can be applied in a Christian way. What we must beware of is trying to establish our case by violence and defamation of character. The way of the cross is not the way of violence and hatred, but it may very well entail nonviolent resistance. Moreover, we should seek to bring pressure to bear out of love and a genuine concern for social justice. Martin Luther King has demonstrated that love and power are not antipodes, but power must be channeled in such a way that the rights of all men are respected. We do not agree with Saul Alinsky that any means are justified in accomplishing worthy social goals. In the attempt to correct social abuses one must take care not to serve a cultural ideology but the gospel of God.

The churches as such should not become agencies of political decision making, but they can lay the foundation for political action through study groups and even public lectures on controversial questions that involve the whole community. As has been said in another chapter, no church should have a prayer group unless it also sponsors a social action cell, for prayer and worldly need must be conjoined. There are occasions, however, when, all other resources having failed and the state itself having fallen under the demonic powers, the church must resort to direct political action. Surely those churches in Germany were justified when they defied the edict of Hitler's government against the deportation of the Jews and sought to hide them and conduct them to safety.

## THE MISSION OF THE CHURCH

One cannot perceive social action in its proper context unless he has a clear understanding of the mission of the church. It is well to remember that the mission of the church is essentially spiritual, that it concerns a kingdom that is not of this world (Jn. 18:36). The great commission was to proclaim the Gospel to the whole creation and to make disciples, teaching them to observe all that Christ commanded (Mk. 16:15; Mt. 28:19, 20). Surely social action is related both to proclamation and discipleship, but understood as a political program of action it should be seen as a fruit and consequence of the mission of the church rather than an integral element in this mission. It is well to bear in mind that neither Jesus nor Paul initiated a program for social change. They concentrated upon the changing of men rather than of social conditions. As Bonhoeffer has said, "Instead of the solution of problems, Jesus brings the redemption of men, and yet for that very reason He does really bring the solution of all human problems as well...but from quite a different plane."[9] What the New Testament does is to lay the foundations for social justice and worldly peace, and Christians are free by the grace of God to apply themselves to these problems. And yet Christians will have quite different aims and motivations from the natural man in the area of social welfare. The Christian will seek not to build the kingdom of God on earth but rather to give glory to God by pointing the world to the eschatological kingdom. He will recognize that civil laws do not change the heart of man but that they can restrain the immoralities of man. The Christian like the enlightened secularist will support those measures which seek to alleviate human misery and poverty. Yet he will recognize that the deepest misery is spiritual and that this can be cured only by a living faith in Jesus Christ. The welfare states of certain Scandinavian countries today with their spiraling suicide and alcoholism rates testify to the fact that material prosperity and security do not solve the problems that plague man's soul. Both men and nations need to be confronted with the reality of God's revelation in Jesus Christ and of His impending judgment. This is where the church makes its unique contribution.

Yet in upholding the spiritual mission of the church we must be careful not to separate this mission from the temporal needs and concerns of men. The church has a spiritual mission, but it is to be lived out in the world. As Emmanuel Mounier, the French personalist, declares: "...since the Church, in imitation of her Master, is fully incarnate, her mission, which is not of this world, must be accomplished in this world."[10] We should not seek to escape from the secular into the spiritual but rather to bring the spiritual to bear on the secular. The Christian ideal is a holiness in the world, which should be distinguished from both the unholy this-worldliness of modern secularism and an ethereal otherworldliness of a certain type of mysticism. We concur in the judgment of William Penn: "True godliness does not

[9] Dietrich Bonhoeffer, *Ethics*, ed. Eberhard Bethge (N.Y.: Macmillan, 1965), p. 355.

[10] Emmanuel Mounier, "Christian Faith and Civilization" in E. Mounier, *Spoil of the Violent* (West Nyack, N.Y.: *Cross Currents*, 1961), p. 16.

turn men out of the world but enables them to live better in it, and excites their endeavors to mend it."[11]

In seeking to realize its mission within the world the church must remember that both its weapons and its goals are spiritual. The kingdom of God cannot be defended by the sword (Mt. 26:51, 52; Lk. 9:54, 55). Nations since they include both the partly regenerate and the unregenerate are permitted to maintain themselves by the sword (Rom. 13:4), but needless cruelty and wanton killing are prohibited by Scriptural law. The nations, which are under God, are allowed to use force to maintain order and secure freedom for their people, but they have no right to play God and to demand from their subjects an absolute obedience which is to be given to God alone. The role of the church is to give spiritual and moral guidance to the leaders of the nations concerning the dire problems of the world, but the church should not try to become a policy-making body, since this is a prerogative that belongs to government. God rules the church by His right hand and the state by His left hand (Luther), and both should therefore refrain from arrogating to themselves absolute authority and power.

The quest for peace is probably the commanding issue of our time. Because it has spiritual as well as purely political implications, both church and state have an obligation to speak on this issue. In seeking for peace we must not isolate it from justice and freedom. As Pope John so poignantly expressed it: ". . . peace will be but an empty-sounding word unless it is founded . . . on truth, built according to justice, vivified and integrated by charity, and put into practice in freedom."[12] At the same time we should recognize that true peace is always an ideal and never a present reality. Augustine observed that the only viable peace in this world is either an uneasy armistice or a Roman peace. In seeking for peace we must remember that it is a gift of God and that it will not become a permanent reality until the coming again of Christ in power and glory. The church can perform a service to the state by reminding it of this truth, because the most dangerous form of political policy is utopianism whereby the state assumes that it can build the perfect society on earth. Both church and state should look beyond this world to the coming kingdom of God in which sacred and

---

11 Quoted in William J. Whalen, *The Quakers* (Chicago: Claretian Publications, 1966), p. 29.
12 *Pacem In Terris,* ed. William J. Gibbons (N.Y.: Paulist Press, 1963), No. 167, p. 57.

secular will finally be united in an enduring synthesis and in which reconciliation between all peoples will then be an accomplished fact.

It is well to bear in mind that the Gospel gives the ultimate solution to the human predicament, not penultimate solutions. Nevertheless, it throws light upon proximate or penultimate answers and thus contributes indirectly to social reform. While it is imperative that we not confuse the righteousness of the kingdom with social justice and the Gospel proclamation with a political platform, it is also necessary that these should always be integrally related.

# FOURTEEN:

# CHRISTIAN UNITY

## THE MOVEMENT FOR REUNION

It is becoming increasingly clear that there cannot be authentic Christian renewal in our time apart from the reunion of the churches. Moreover, the final reunion of the severed branches of Christendom cannot take place apart from spiritual renewal. It was the prayer of our Lord that all of His children be one (Jn. 17:20, 21). Paul proclaimed that there is only one body, one Spirit, one Lord, one faith and one baptism (Eph. 4:4, 5). It is a scandal that the body of Christ has been rent asunder, that obedience has been demanded to confessional formulas rather than to the one faith into which we were baptized. It is also shocking that all Christians do not acknowledge a common baptism, even though only the one baptism with water and the Spirit is recognized by our Lord.

The disunity of the churches is a grave obstacle to the task of evangelizing the world. There can indeed be no finally compelling witness to Christ unless this is a united witness. Christian missionaries have complained of the scandal on the mission field, of how missionaries from the different churches are competing against one another for converts rather than upholding Jesus Christ as their common Lord and Savior. Richard Baxter has surely asked a pertinent question: "Has anything in the world done more to lose our authority and disable us for God's service, than our differences and divisions?"[1]

The ecumenical movement arose partly to overcome the sectarianism and divisiveness of the churches. The word ecumenical is derived from the Greek *oikumene,* meaning "world." An ecumenical theology is one that includes the whole church throughout the entire world. Ecumenism has been born out of the realization that the era of denominations is over. Those who have been in the vanguard of this movement have seen that burgeoning denominational bureaucracies have stood in the way

---

[1] Richard Baxter, *The Reformed Pastor,* ed. J. T. Wilkinson (London: Epworth, 1950), 2nd ed. rev., p. 124.

of effective Christian witness and need to be supplanted by new structures that can pool the resources of the various churches for the work of mission and evangelism.

The body of Christ is broken, but it is not really divided. As Christians we already have an essential spiritual unity in Christ. But we must seek to give visible expression to this unity. We are beneficiaries of the unity that the apostles experienced at Pentecost, but we must try to realize this unity concretely in our ecclesiastical life. Christian unity is both a gift and a task. It has been assured to us by the act of God in Christ and the outpouring of the Holy Spirit upon the church. But it must be appropriated and realized in a worldwide fellowship of faith and love that cuts across all racial and class lines and that is bound together by an eternal Gospel and common sacraments.

The two sides of ecumenism are the catholic and the evangelical. The catholic element connotes universality and continuity with the tradition. It is marked by an appreciation for the works of grace and the means of grace which are the traditional emphases of the church. The evangelical side signifies an emphasis on the message of free grace and the necessity to receive this by faith alone. The term evangelical also includes the connotation of outreaching, bringing the message to all peoples and nations. A truly ecumenical church will be both catholic and evangelical, and indeed this was the original intention and goal of the Protestant Reformation.

Full Christian unity entails more than Catholic-Protestant reunion. It includes also reunion with the Eastern Orthodox churches and the small sects. It will even involve the reconciliation of Christians and Jews under the cross of Christ. Indeed, the first break in the church occurred between the church and the synagogue, and this rupture will be the most difficult to heal.

## FALSE ECUMENICITY

In the quest for Christian unity one must be on guard against a false ecumenism by which the tenets of the faith itself are compromised. One of the chief perils is eclecticism which means drawing from a variety of religious traditions in order to arrive at a common truth or experience. Some theologians who have been active in the ecumenical movement have sought to look beyond the historic Christian faith to a new religious synthesis which incorporates the best components of all the major religions. Paul Tillich, for example, speaks of the "Religion of the

Concrete Spirit" which he believes will supersede institutional Christianity.[2] Such theologians as A. Roy Eckardt and Reinhold Niebuhr underplay the distinctive marks of the Christian revelation as over against the wisdom of ancient Israel and thereby argue against missions to the Jews. Other Protestant scholars in an attempt to facilitate relations with Roman Catholicism have sought to minimize the distinctive contribution of the Reformation and have even discouraged Reformation festivals by which the biblical message of justification is once again brought to the fore. One Protestant seminary in the middle west remarks in its catalogue that we should no longer discuss the issues that divide but only those that unite. But the danger is that by avoiding controversial doctrinal issues we may prepare the way not for the recovery of biblical faith but for an indiscriminate inclusivism which signifies a capitulation to the relativistic spirit of the modern age. Not only Catholics but also Protestants need to pay heed to Pope Paul's warnings against indifferentism and a false irenicism.

Forsyth has rightly reminded us that the search for variety may only mirror modern relativism and not a genuine concern for Christian unity. It is well to note that Schleiermacher was already advocating church unity on the basis not of biblical truth but of a common experience. He remarks: "The visible religious society can only be brought nearer the universal freedom and majestic unity of the true church by becoming a mobile mass, having no distinct outlines, but each part being now here, now there, and all peacefully mingling together."[3] This is not evangelical Christianity but a latitudinarianism which regards all creeds as insignificant. The only sin in this kind of theology is intolerance. We would do well to heed these words of that ecumenical pioneer Nathan Söderblom: "Universalism will be attained more surely through a grasping and developing of the essential than through an embracing of the manifold."[4]

The ecumenical movement at its best contains a note of exclusiveness. Jesus Christ is regarded as the only foundation for unity. The ecumenical venture is open to all, but it is also

---

2 Paul Tillich, *The Future of Religions* (N.Y.: Harper & Row, 1965), pp. 87-89.

3 Friedrich Schleiermacher, *On Religion*, trans. John Oman (N.Y.: Harper & Row, 1958), p. 175.

4 See Gustaf Aulén, "Nathan Söderblom As Theologian" in *Una Sancta*, Vol. 24, No. 1 (Resurrection, 1967), (pp. 15-30), p. 30.

demanding of all. It demands nothing less than total commitment to the risen Lord, Jesus Christ. True ecumenicity is just the opposite of eclecticism and syncretism. This is made very clear by Dr. Visser 't Hooft, the former president of the World Council of Churches, in his book *No Other Name*.[5] He makes a sharp contrast between the various forms of religious syncretism and Christian universalism. Forsyth, one of the precursors of the ecumenical movement, declared: "A Gospel which is not exclusive will never include the world, for it will never master it. No religion will include devotees which does not exclude rivals."[6]

Against those who would compromise the faith in an attempt to improve relations with fellow religionists, we hold that ecumenicity signifies the unity of love and truth. There can be no reunion of the churches apart from a common confession. The COCU plan of union which seeks to unite ten churches in this country is hampered by the fact that it seeks organic union before doctrinal agreement.[7] It makes a place for creeds but interprets them only as symbols of the faith of past ages rather than as a binding word from God for our time. The danger in COCU is that the participating churches may end in acknowledging many creeds but subscribing to none.[8] Karl Barth has said that sometimes it is necessary to oppose particular mergers so that unity might be attained on a deeper level. The ultimate goal of the ecumenical movement is to include the whole world under the banner of Jesus Christ. Ecumenism should therefore be seen as primarily a missionary movement, and this means fidelity to the Word of God in Holy Scripture. COCU may yet prove to be a work of the Spirit of God, and one should be open to this bold plan for Christian unity even while criticizing the way in which many of the church leaders seek to realize it.

Another spurious form of ecumenism is what might be termed organizationalism or churchly ecumenism. Here the concern is for institutional mergers which have as their goal greater efficiency and deeper influence upon the culture. Some proponents

---

[5] W. A. Visser 't Hooft, *No Other Name* (Philadelphia: Westminster, 1963).

[6] P. T. Forsyth, *The Church and the Sacraments*, 2nd ed. (London: Independent Press, 1947), p. 18.

[7] COCU signifies The Consultation on Church Union and includes among the participating churches the Methodist, the United Presbyterian, the Episcopal and the United Church of Christ.

[8] For a poignant critique of COCU see James Boice, " 'I Believe in COCU'?" in *Christianity Today*, Vol. XI, No. 15 (April 18, 1967), pp. 3-6.

of churchly ecumenism envisage a super-church with its own board of directors, a uniform liturgy, a common polity and a centralized administrative apparatus. One variation of this kind of ecumenism is denominational imperialism whereby a denomination seeks to advance itself through institutional merger. The recent Methodist-Evangelical United Brethren merger is sometimes given as an example of denominational imperialism. The COCU plan of union is also possibly open to the charge of churchly ecumenism and even imperialism; yet we must recognize that it seeks a pattern of church organization which surmounts racial and class barriers and also which marks the death of denominational structures. What is needed is not simply a more efficient organization but another Pentecost which pours new life into the structures of the church. The goal of authentic ecumenism is not a super-church with power and prestige but rather a worldwide fellowship of believers united under the Word and dedicated to the conversion and salvation of mankind. What we should aim for is not churchly ecumenism but an evangelical ecumenism which places Christian mission above institutional survival.

Many theologians and scholars today are defending what is now being called secular ecumenism. In this view the way in which unity is realized is by participation in common tasks in the world. It is said that our unity is in our service rather than in doctrine. We contend, however, that Christian unity means something much more than a unity in function; it surely entails a common faith and a common Lord. The basis of our unity is not service to the world; rather outgoing service is a consequence and evidence of our common faith in Jesus Christ. Our unity as Christians springs not from our common humanity but from God's act of reconciliation in Jesus Christ.

An opposite danger is spiritual ecumenism in which the emphasis is on unity in spirit but not in body or organization. We maintain that Christian unity in the Scriptural sense will be both spiritual and visible. It will not only entail unity in faith but a visible fellowship of love which is the concrete expression of this faith. Indeed, there cannot be any real unity among Christians until our churches are open to all persons notwithstanding racial or denominational background. Spiritual ecumenism by itself is a false ecumenicity because this means that race, class and denominational barriers still remain. There can be church union without spiritual unity, but there cannot be authentic spiritual unity apart from some kind of federation

and/or union of the churches. But this does not imply a monolithic structure with a hierarchy of bishops and centralized control. A united fellowship of Christians will allow for diversity
within unity, and this diversity should even extend to liturgy,
Sunday School curriculum, and evangelistic strategy.

Finally we need to warn against both Catholic and Evangelical triumphalism whereby we seek to impose our particular
confessional views upon others. The way to unity according to
the triumphalist mentality lies in conversion to a particular
confession. The Catholic triumphalist will sound the call back
to Rome, whereas his Evangelical counterpart will seek a re-
pristination of Calvin, Luther or simply confessional orthodoxy.
Both parties are blind to the sins of their own churches and are
only too ready to find fault with other church bodies. The way
to reunion lies not in conversion but in convergence, in the
strengthening and flowering in all churches of those elements
that are rooted in the Gospel. We espouse not a return to Rome
or Geneva or Wittenberg but a breakthrough into a new form of
the church. Not the church of the past but the coming great
church should be our vision and hope. And the best way to
realize this vision is by each church seeking to reform itself in
the light of the Gospel.

The final goal of the ecumenical movement is not denominational unity or even Christian unity but the conversion of the
whole world to Jesus Christ. Christian unity must serve the cause
of Christian mission. As our Lord Himself declared: "I pray
... that they may all be one ... so that the world may believe
that thou hast sent me" (Jn. 17:20, 21). That the note of
evangelism is lacking in the conciliar movement is surely something to be deplored.

Max Lackmann, former president of the League for Evangeli-
cal-Catholic Reunion, has stressed the need for the corporate reunion of the Evangelical churches with the Roman Catholic
church. But he seeks for union without prior doctrinal agreement, and this may be a serious error. The reintegration of
Protestantism within the Roman church, as envisioned by Lackmann, would surely entail an hierarchical institution and very
probably the papacy as well. But papacy and hierarchy are not
the only options open for those who seek church unity. Eastern
Orthodox Christianity has shown in its concept of autocephalous
churches that there can be both spiritual and visible unity apart
from a monolithic structure. This does not necessarily mean
that the papacy would be completely out of the picture in a

unified Christian church, but it would without doubt be a transformed papacy. The pope would possibly be seen not as a monarch nor as an infallible teacher but as a presiding bishop in a college of bishops that would hopefully be elected by the laity.

Our recommendation is for church union in stages. We need first to bind up the wounds within the evangelical churches before we can think seriously of corporate union with the Roman Catholic church or the Eastern churches. Christian unity will be a facade if we unite with Rome and remain estranged from the Pentecostals, the Nazarenes, the Seventh-Day Adventists, the Bible churches and others of the "third force" who comprise the growing edge of Protestantism. It is a step forward that we are now able to address our Catholic friends as "brethren," but we in the mainstream of Protestantism have yet to extend the hand of fellowship and reconciliation to our Pentecostal and Holiness brethren. Dr. John Mackay is among the few who are seeking to overcome the barriers that separate the established historic churches of Protestantism from the third force Protestants. But we should not rest content with Protestant unity; rather we should press on to world Christian unity. The goal of ecumenism is not a Pan-Protestantism but the reconciliation and reunion of all members and branches of the Holy Catholic Church.

## CATHOLIC EVANGELICALISM

The kind of theology that we should seek is one that is both profoundly evangelical and authentically catholic. It might be termed an evangelical ecumenism or better a catholic evangelicalism. The goal of such a theology would not simply be the unity of the church but also and above all the conversion of the world. It is well to note that the Protestant Reformers wished to be Evangelical Catholics. They did not desire to create a new church but rather to reform and purify the old church. Yet they were not able to carry out their program apart from a break with the papacy and the Roman church. Nevertheless in the early days of the Reformation many Reformed churches still called themselves Catholic churches.

Dr. Pelikan has wisely termed the Reformation a tragedy as well as a necessity.[9] It was a tragedy because it signified the rupture and division of Christendom. It was necessary because the

9 Jaroslav Pelikan, *The Riddle of Roman Catholicism* (Nashville: Abingdon, 1959), pp. 45-57.

message of free grace could not find a safe anchorage in the Roman church of that time. Since the Reformation the two great branches of Christendom have become increasingly defensive. The fidelity of Protestantism was transferred from the Gospel to the letter of the Bible and thereby the evangelical element was obscured. The Counter-Reformation within Catholicism placed ever greater authority upon the church as an institution and thereby the Roman church has come to represent the confinement of catholicity.[10]

This brings us to the truth that one cannot be fully evangelical without at the same time being truly catholic. And one cannot be catholic without also being evangelical. The hallmark of evangelicalism is the message of free grace, but free grace becomes cheap grace if it is not associated with the demand for discipleship and holiness which characterizes catholocism. The catholic emphasis on the holy life on the other hand soon becomes works-righteousness unless it is solidly anchored in the evangelical message of justification. Evangelicals have likewise stressed the necessity for personal repentance and faith. It is said that we receive the grace of God by faith alone *(sola fide)*. Yet the life of faith cannot maintain itself apart from the sacraments which are again a catholic concern. Evangelicals uphold the justification of the ungodly whereas Catholics have traditionally concentrated upon the sanctification of the righteous. Yet justification apart from sanctification is exclusively forensic and thereby abstract and external. Sanctification apart from justification soon degenerates into moralism and legalism. The catholic and evangelical strands are two notes in the Christian symphony, and both are indispensable.

The Christian church should ideally be a coat of many colors. It should make room for the diversity of gifts and ministries of which Paul speaks (cf. Rom. 12:3-8; I Cor. 12; Eph. 4:11-16). We concur in this statement of Pierre Emery: "The unity of the Body of Christ does not spring from a levelling of persons, but on the contrary, comes into being through the very diversity of personal *charismas*."[11] The church is under one Lord, Jesus Christ, and it proclaims one message, the Gospel of reconciliation and redemption. But there should be room for various interpretations and creedal formulations. Whether the church

---

10 See Bela Vassady, *Christ's Church: Evangelical, Catholic, and Reformed* (Grand Rapids: Eerdmans, 1965), pp. 19-22.

11 Pierre-Yves Emery, *The Communion of Saints,* trans. D. J. and M. Watson (London: Faith Press, 1966), p. 77.

of the future should have a visible as well as a spiritual head is a matter of conjecture. Protestant scholars such as Cullmann are now agreed that Jesus probably made Peter the visible head of the New Testament church, but this does not imply that his prerogatives could be passed on to successors.[12] The unity and integrity of the church must not be located in its ministry or order but rather in its Gospel. Only when we awaken to this truth can a church structure be formed that is in full accord with Holy Scripture.

In this ecumenical age it is necessary to affirm both the sinfulness and the holiness of the church. The church that has no stain or blemish (Eph. 5:27) should be seen as an eschatological reality. It was Thomas Aquinas who remarked:

> That the Church may be glorious, without spot or wrinkle, is the final goal to which we are being led through the passion of Christ. It will be so only in our eternal home, not on our journey there, during which, if we said we had no sin, we should be deceiving ourselves, as we are told in the First Epistle of John.[13]

The church can be regarded as indefectible in the sense that it cannot finally be overthrown (Mt. 16:18), but it should not be upheld as infallible. Its Lord is infallible, its message is infallible, the truth which it conveys by the Spirit is infallible, but its own formulations and interpretations are only approximations of the truth and need constantly to be sharpened and even corrected.

Likewise we need once again to recover the truth of the divine inspiration of Scriptures, but this should not be made to imply total inerrancy. Holy Scripture is the infallible rule for faith and practice, but it is not to be seen as a perfect measuring rod on matters of secular history and science. The Bible is an earthen vessel which carries the treasure of eternal salvation, and such a vessel necessarily reflects the cultural limitations of the times in which it was written. At the same time it is not a broken vessel, since it has been inspired by the Spirit, and this means that it is able to bear and convey the truth of revelation. Our view is that Scripture contains the authentic interpretation of the saving events which it mirrors. The Bible comes prior to the church in that its revelatory message has its origin in God. But the church is prior to the Bible insofar as it was the church that com-

---

12 See Oscar Cullmann, *Peter* (Philadelphia: Westminster, 1953).

13 Thomas Aquinas, *Summa Theologica*, Part III, q. 8, a. 3, ad 2. Trans. in H. Küng, *That the World May Believe* (N.Y.: Sheed & Ward, 1963), p. 34.

piled and recognized the books of the Bible as authoritative and sacred. At the same time we believe as Protestants that it is the Spirit who authorized and created the canon; the church simply recognized and confirmed the divine work of the Spirit. A catholic evangelical theology would hold not only to the Word within the church but also to the church under the Word.

The marks of the church have traditionally been understood in Reformation Protestantism as the Word and the sacraments. But should not we add a mark that was surely stressed in the New Testament — the Christian life? Jesus said that His disciples would be recognized on the basis of how they loved one another (cf. Jn. 13:35; 15:8-10). It might be said that the church is not only where the Word is proclaimed and celebrated but also where it is obeyed. A catholic evangelicalism will also be an evangelical devotionism, since Christian truth cannot live apart from Christian devotion. We concur with many of the secular theologians today that what is needed is a Christian style of life, but we should quickly add that such a style of life must be grounded in Scripture and nurtured within the church.

As has been said Christian unity is a gift, but it is also a task, a calling. Joseph Sittler has remarked that unity will be given by Christ when Christians become obedient to His will and sensitive to reality.[14] Protestants need to move from an anarchic liberalism and insularized conservatism towards a catholic evangelicalism. Roman Catholics need to move from a narrow Romanism and objectivistic sacramentalism to an evangelical catholicism. We should aim not for the synthesis of Evangelical and Roman Catholic thought and practice but rather for their mutual purification in the light of the Word of God so that what is authentically evangelical and catholic might come to the fore.

Charles Spurgeon has declared: "I am quite sure that the best way to promote union is to promote truth. It will not do for us to be all united together by yielding to one another's mistakes."[15] These remarks contain much wisdom, but we must go on to affirm that one should speak the truth in love. We cannot finally arrive at truth if we are estranged from one another, if we refuse to receive one another as brothers. Archbishop Athenagoras, the Eastern Orthodox patriarch, has rightly discerned that a dialogue of charity must precede theological dialogue.

---

[14] In an address at Clarke College, Dubuque, Iowa, Nov. 3, 1966.
[15] Quoted in *The Presbyterian Journal*, Vol. XXVI, No. 25 (Oct. 18, 1967), p. 15.

Moreover, we should also speak the truth in humility knowing that we share in the guilt of discord and schism within the church. We as Protestants must approach our Catholic and Orthodox brethren in the knowledge that our fathers have also been guilty of mistakes and even crimes in the name of religion. The way to Christian unity is the way of repentance under the cross of Christ.

# INDEX OF SUBJECTS

# INDEX OF NAMES

# INDEX OF SCRIPTURE